W9-DEA-764

# HIGHER EDUCATION AND THE NEW SOCIETY

GEORGE KELLER

THE JOHNS HOPKINS UNIVERSITY PRESS
*Baltimore*

© 2008 The Johns Hopkins University Press
All rights reserved. Published 2008
Printed in the United States of America on acid-free paper
2 4 6 8 9 7 5 3 1

The Johns Hopkins University Press
2715 North Charles Street
Baltimore, Maryland 21218-4363
www.press.jhu.edu

Library of Congress Cataloging-in-Publication Data

Keller, George, 1928–2007
Higher education and the new society / George Keller.
p. cm.
Includes bibliographical references and index.
ISBN-13: 978-0-8018-9031-4 (hardcover : alk. paper)
ISBN-10: 0-8018-9031-4 (hardcover : alk. paper)
1. Education, Higher—Aims and objectives—United States.
2. Education, Higher—Social aspects—United States.
3. Educational change—United States.  I. Title.
LA227.4.K455 2008
379.73—dc22     2008007843

A catalog record for this book is available from the British Library.

*Special discounts are available for bulk purchases of this book. For
more information, please contact Special Sales at 410-516-6936 or
specialsales@press.jhu.edu.*

The Johns Hopkins University Press uses environmentally
friendly book materials, including recycled text paper that is
composed of at least 30 percent post-consumer waste, whenever possible. All of our book papers are acid-free, and our
jackets and covers are printed on paper with recycled content.

For
ELISABETH KATHERINE KICKELHEIN KELLER
(1899–1995)

NOTE: George Keller wrote most of this book while being treated for leukemia at the Sidney Kimmel Comprehensive Cancer Center at the Johns Hopkins Hospital. His gratitude for superb care extended to all the doctors, nurses, pharmacists, phlebotomists, and uncountable others he came to know there. But he wished particularly to acknowledge three people whose skill and attentiveness gave him the time and strength to keep working. Lee Resta, M.D., senior fellow in oncology, was unfailingly responsive, resourceful, and energetic. Mary Beth Halter, B.S.N., R.N., was a constant source of expertise, intelligence, and good cheer. And Mary Beth Collins, B.S.N., R.N., involved herself, often voluntarily, in every aspect of George's care. Their hopefulness and helpfulness, in themselves, were excellent medicine. All the words in this or any other book would not be enough to convey adequate thanks or appreciation.                *Jane Eblen Keller*

# CONTENTS

# PREFACE

---

In recent years criticisms of America's colleges and universities have been the harshest in a half century, and calls for reform and restructuring of U.S. higher education have reached a crescendo.

> We believe that what is called for in higher education is nothing less than a complete restructuring of universities, including the way they are organized, the way undergraduates are taught, and the substance of the curriculum.[1]

> Our basic organizational structures are no longer adequate for social or educational needs. They resist shifting human and material resources across departmental lines . . . We need a new structure inside the university that actually meets the needs of those whom we are serving.[2]

> The colleges that survive will be those that change in a fundamental way, that figure out how to restructure the delivery of their curriculum and administrative services at less cost without sacrificing quality.[3]

> The question is no longer whether to retract, consolidate, restructure, and adapt in order to bear down on

the basic mission of higher education—preparing students to take part in their civilization—but whether these reforms can be accomplished from within or must be imposed from without.[4]

This is only a quartet of quotations from concerned higher education insiders. The comments of many outsiders—business and government leaders and a swelling segment of the public—sometimes border on the scurrilous.

How justified are these suggestions and demands for fundamental changes at America's colleges and universities? After all, numerous observers from C. P. Snow on have said that U.S. higher education is one of the glories of the modern world. Why are so many intelligent persons suddenly calling for radical alterations? And why is it so difficult for most academic institutions to adjust? Also, exactly how should universities restructure themselves?

This book is an effort to answer these and allied questions. If higher education is now the main engine of economic growth, personal opportunity, and social harmony, its current condition should be accurately appraised, and the forces that compel structural renovations should be thoroughly understood. Only then will colleges and universities be able to undertake the proper kinds of changes.

The demands that American colleges and universities change their ways are understandable because the nation has changed considerably. We have become a conspicuously different society in the past three decades. People in the United States have been living through a revolution in values, finances, behavior, technology, and education since the 1970s. This upheaval constitutes the most consequential set of changes in society since the late nineteenth century, when the nation went from a largely domestic, rural, agrarian mode of living to an industrial, international, and urban economy, and when small, often religious colleges evolved into larger, secular colleges and embryonically great universities.[5] In several ways, we have become a new America. Clearly, colleges and universities cannot continue to act as they did before the 1970s.

It therefore seems imperative that everyone concerned about U.S. higher education recognize two things: that the society has been going through revolutionary changes and that new, outside forces require educators to rethink and redesign some of their operations. (The late Lawrence Cremin, perhaps the finest historian and most clairvoyant analyst of schools in the past century, pointed to the urgency of these two recognitions in his remarkable little book, *Public Education*.)[6]

It would be prudent if higher education's enlarging cadre of critics stopped bashing colleges and universities as if the institutions had not already made numerous changes and as if the colleges and universities were not themselves being buffeted and made convulsive by the societal revolution of the past three decades. It is a popular sport in the United States to castigate schools and colleges; critics seem to imagine that students and classes are immune to powerful new forces such as broken and fatherless families, television, urban crime and violence, drugs, computers, and rock music. In a crazy compliment to the field of education, many people seem to believe that, if only we had better teaching, an improved curriculum, and greater accountability, schools and colleges could transform the country's health, manners, economy, and behavior. The faith is touching but bizarre.

Colleges and universities can and do, of course, help shape the outlines of modern civilization. Indeed, a considerable portion of our substantially new society has been shaped by institutions of higher education and their graduates. But colleges are, to an appallingly unperceived extent, also shaped by the society outside their leafy campuses. That canny education observer K. Patricia Cross has seen this clearly: "Most change in higher education comes from forces external to the institution—factors such as the demographics of the birth rate, migration patterns, directives from the state board of education, sweeping court decisions, shifts in the job markets, and the like. These external pressures for change are sufficient now to call for a new lens through which to view the role of higher education in society."[7]

The intent of this book is to describe the outside changes in American society that are eroding the traditional hillocks of college and university life and to delineate the internal changes in higher education that have quietly taken place in response to the new and turbulent environment. Believe it or not, most colleges and universities have already altered their operations far more than most people, including many in higher education, realize. But I will also attempt, apprehensively, to point to some additional changes and basic restructuring that might be considered by college and university leaders and faculties and by their governmental and foundation supporters. Change in higher education can no longer be incremental. It must be fundamental and structural.

IN THE PREPARATION OF THIS BOOK I was aided at the beginning by a small grant from the Carnegie Corporation of New York, which enabled me to excavate data on what was happening in American society and within higher education. Then the Pew Charitable Trusts generously provided funds for travel to numerous colleges and universities, for study, and for writing. To both benefactors I express my huge appreciation and gratitude.

I was also aided by interviews and discussions—full of ideas, insights, and information—with some of America's keenest scholars and actors in higher education. Alphabetically, these include David Adamany, James Appleberry, Alexander Astin, the late Ernest Boyer, David Breneman, John Burness, Ronald Calgaard, Richard Chait, Charles Clotfelter, George Connick, K. Patricia Cross, Gordon Davies, Richard Dober, Rhoda Dorsey, James Duderstadt, Donald Eastman, Judith Eaton, Elaine El-Khawas, Martin Finkelstein, Richard Freeland, Stanley Gabor, Kay Hanson, Ira Harkavy, Robert Hetterick, D. Bruce Johnstone, Jeffrey Kittay, Donald Langenberg, George LaNoue, Clara Lovett, Theodore Marchese, Wilfred McClay, Michael McPherson, James Mingle, James Morrison, Steven Muller, Barry Munitz, Michael Nettles, Michael Olivas, Marvin Peterson, R. Eugene Rice, Richard Ruch, Harold Shapiro, Robert Shirley, Rebecca Stafford, John Thelin, Vincent Tinto, and David Webster.

I also benefited greatly and often from the advice of my professorial wife, Jane, whose sanity and wisdom about higher learning match my fascination with the enterprise.

HIGHER EDUCATION
AND THE NEW SOCIETY

# THE INGREDIENTS
# OF THE NEW SOCIETY

As our case is new, so we must think anew, and act
anew. We must disenthrall ourselves.

ABRAHAM LINCOLN

A definitive study [of universities] calls first of all for a
clear description of the essential characteristics of our
age and an accurate diagnosis of the rising generation.

JOSÉ ORTEGA Y GASSET

O N OCTOBER 16, 1959, a thirty-seven-year-old scholar
of early American history delivered a paper that
stunned the twenty-one other noted scholars who had
gathered for the Conference on Early American Education at Williamsburg, Virginia. The historian was Bernard
Bailyn of Harvard, and his paper was subsequently published, along with a superlative bibliographical essay, as
a small book, *Education in the Forming of American Society*.[1] Though the appellation is sometimes exaggerated,
Bailyn's was a seminal essay.

Bailyn called it "an essay in hypothetical history" in

which he attempted to "tell a different and I think more useful kind of story about education than those we are accustomed to hear" (5). His view was different, he wrote, because he sought to replace the traditional scholarship about education in the United States with a new scholarship that looked at educational forces in their full social and historical context. To Bailyn the historical writing about and analysis of education in America was peculiar. "Its leading characteristic is its separateness as a branch of history, its detachment from the main stream of historical research, writing, and teaching. It is a distinct tributary" (5). He worried that this scholarly isolation was crippling; "We have almost no historical leverage on the problems of American education" (4). Bailyn observed about those who studied education that

they directed their attention almost exclusively to the part of the educational process carried on in formal institutions of instruction. They spoke of schools as self-contained entities whose development had followed an inner logic and innate propulsion . . . [and] they lost the capacity to see [education] in its full context and hence to assess the variety and magnitude of the burdens it has borne and to judge its historical importance (9).

Bailyn thought that this confined preoccupation of educationists had stunted the growth of education as a scholarly field. "The more parochial the subject became, the less capable it was of attracting the kinds of scholars who could give it broad relevance and bring it back into the public domain" (9). The young historian suggested that education needed to be understood as the panoply of ideas, skills, morals, attitudes, information, behaviors, and methods that each generation handed down to its successor generation, as well as the historical, economic, and cultural reasons that a people taught its young what it did and how it did it. To Bailyn there is much more to education—to cultivating, training, and shaping children and adolescents—than what is taught in schools and colleges. Bernard Bailyn reminded his audience that, for the early settlers of colonial America, "the most important agency in the transfer of culture . . . was the family" (15). Children were educated mostly at home. Churches, local communities, apprenticeships, laws, and the rigors of life in the wilderness of the new land also helped form young people's manners, morals, work habits, knowledge, and allegiances. Only later in the colonial period did elementary schools and a few tiny, new colleges like Harvard and William and Mary begin to help educate as well.

Bailyn's call to expand the purview of thinking and study about education has largely been ignored, as were John Dewey's earlier attempts to connect education with the emerging industrial, scientific society.[2] Dewey had warned that, "when the schools depart from the educational conditions effective in the out-of-school environment, they necessarily substitute a bookish, pseudo-intellectual spirit for a social spirit."[3] From the plethora of reports about America such as the extravagant national commission appraisal of 1983, *A Nation at Risk: The Imperative for Educational Reform,* to most of the current scholarship and commentary about U.S. colleges and universities, today's outlook on education and ideas for reform are still remarkably insular.

True, there have been some exceptions in the field of higher education studies, such as the writings of Daniel

Bell,[4] James S. Coleman,[5] Richard Hofstadter,[6] Clark Kerr,[7] David Riesman,[8] and Martin Trow.[9] But much of the scholarship and lay criticism of higher learning in the United States still view the enterprise as one largely sheltered from outside changes and only weakly influential in reshaping America's social structure. This situation is both baffling and worrisome.

It is baffling because, since Plato wrote *The Republic* nearly twenty-four hundred years ago, most intelligent people have been aware of the intricate connection between the aspirations and structure of a society and the education that its people receive. And in the United States, Thomas Jefferson, Horace Mann, John Dewey, and Lawrence Cremin, among numerous others, have reminded citizens about the close interplay between the economy and culture and the behavior, morals, and education of youth.

It is baffling also because more than a few of today's critics of higher education lament that technology has changed, the economy has changed, families have changed, religious values have changed, race relations have changed, and the composition of the population has changed but U.S. colleges and universities have remained relatively unchanged. Reasonable persons might conclude that scholars and leaders of education would therefore concentrate on the ways that recent social changes affect and possibly should reconfigure collegiate education and on how higher learning can continue to contribute to changes in the nation.

The isolated thinking about schools and colleges is worrisome because Americans may be living in a time of transformation almost as momentous as that which faced the European settlers and African slave laborers who had to adjust to a very different life on the strange, wild continent—the invented social world that historian Bailyn described so cogently. If this is so, it seems urgent that professionals in higher education should understand and appraise the nature of American society's current transformation and adjust university structures and content in a beneficial Darwinian way.

The social transformation is of two kinds. One has been building for a century and a half. This gradual, long-term metamorphosis was portrayed best and often by the late James S. Coleman, one of America's greatest sociologists of education.[10] Enlightenment ideas, the industrial revolution, stronger national and state government, the advance of science and technology, expanding welfare policies, new forms of transportation, the women's movement, computers and television, and the spread of expressive individualism[11] as a central value have all contributed to moving social life away from extended families, churches and synagogues, small towns, agriculture, local commerce and community activities, crafts and small businesses, social hierarchies, and self-reliance and toward large cities, corporations, universities and governments, liberated individualism, increased mobility and international trade, greater equality of gender, race, and ethnicity, dependence on numerous entitlement programs, lessened moral taboos, and e-mail and Web pages. As James S. Coleman observed, "The social capital on which primordial social organization depends for social control has been eroded."

The social capital to develop children and young women and men, or the several means of education to produce excellent human capital much as land, labor, equipment, and management produce economic capital, has changed profoundly during the past century. We live in a vastly different educational world from that of the colonial parents and offspring described by Bernard Bailyn. Family guidance is less, and peer, media, and gang guidance is more.[12] The young now heed radio, television, the Internet, and popular music rather than religious sermons and the advice of community elders. Many youths spend thousands of hours for eleven to twenty-two years in schools of various kinds—preschools, elementary schools, secondary schools, tutorials, colleges, proprietary schools, graduate and professional schools, and continuing education schools—but they read and write less and now sit before a computer much as they once curled up with books, built things, and did family chores. Apprenticeships have almost disappeared; instead, many youths now work at part-time jobs of several kinds, often beginning in secondary school and continuing through doctoral studies in graduate school or advanced studies in law, architecture, or engineering. The way that young people learn has changed radically, and the sources of their education have multiplied.

The other kind of transformation is more recent and has occurred more swiftly. It is actually composed of a collection of fundamental shifts, new conditions, technological innovations, and changing behaviors, many of which began in the late 1960s and 1970s. During those two decades the United States went through changes so substantial that it is possible to claim that Americans have entered a new society. The nation's flavor of life and the character of its higher education are being affected radically.

## Demographics

"The dominant factor for business in the next two decades . . . is not going to be economics or technology. It will be demographics."[13] So said the seldom reticent Peter Drucker. In this he was echoing the observation of John Maynard Keynes, who contended that the great events in history are often the result of slow changes in demography. The United States is certainly going through several major changes demographically, as are many other nations of the world, and these have begun to affect U.S. colleges and universities. Most likely, the changes will influence higher education even more forcefully in the decades ahead.

When the twenty-third General Population Conference was held in Beijing, China, in October 1997, most of the presentations focused on the dangers of overpopulation. But during the past two decades fertility rates—the average number of children born per woman—have been dropping sharply. Except for most countries in Africa and much of the Muslim world in the Middle East and Southeast Asia, birth rates are now declining in nearly every country. In several countries the decline has been amazing. Ireland, for example, had a fertility rate of 3.55 in 1970 but only 1.90 in 2000. (To reproduce a nation's population, a fertility rate of 2.1 is necessary.) China, Taiwan, and South Korea have cut their birth rates in half since 1965. And since 1980, the Chinese, with the aid of ultrasound and amniocentesis, have increased the number of males and reduced the number of females born.[14] In Italy, which has one of the lowest fertility rates in the world, the population of 57 million has already stopped growing, and the government has begun reducing thousands of classes and closing schools. Some demographers predict that, if present trends continue, global depopulation could begin by the year 2050.

This decline in the fertility rate is the most rapid decline in world history. Here are the 2000 fertility rates for twenty-two countries, as reported by the United Nations Population Division's 2002 biennial compendium.

| | | | |
|---|---|---|---|
| China | 1.15 | Britain | 1.70 |
| Czech Republic | 1.18 | France | 1.76 |
| Spain | 1.19 | Australia | 1.77 |
| Italy | 1.21 | Ireland | 1.90 |
| Russia | 1.25 | Thailand | 1.95 |
| Germany | 1.34 | United States | 2.05 |
| Poland | 1.48 | Iran | 2.53 |
| South Korea | 1.51 | Argentina | 2.62 |
| Cuba | 1.55 | Turkey | 2.70 |
| Canada | 1.56 | Mexico | 2.75 |
| Singapore | 1.57 | Israel | 2.94 |

By contrast, most of the African nations, such as Somalia and Uganda, and the Muslim nations, such as Yemen, Afghanistan, and Pakistan, have fertility rates ranging from 5.0 to 8.0.

Why has there been such a decline in births among many developed and several third world nations? There are several reasons. More people are moving into the cities and surrounding suburbs, and children cost more in cities. Contraception methods have improved and are more widely used. The growing opportunities for women in the workplace have reduced the time available to women for child rearing, tending, and training. Also, more women are becoming highly educated, and well-educated women have fewer children than do the less educated. In Colombia, for instance, the best-educated women have three fewer children than do the least educated. Doubtless, housing, changing religious attachments, and other factors contribute to the new fertility rates. But whatever the reasons, the consequences are considerable.

Today's developed nations, including Russia and Japan, house one in four of all people in the world; three decades from now they may house only one in six. Africa alone will have more people than all of North America, Europe, Russia, and Japan combined. Nigeria will have a population density similar to that of Holland today. The population in India could equal that of China, and Pakistan could become the third most populous nation in the world. The gap between rich and poor countries, which already have difficulty feeding themselves, will probably widen further, as may the income gaps within most third world societies. The pressures for immigration to wealthier nations will almost certainly intensify.

Colleges and universities may see a new mix of the approximately six hundred thousand students who enroll annually from abroad, and they will need to pay greater attention to the Muslim and African worlds. They may be pressed to take demography more seriously as one of the social sciences, and they will need to reassess their programs of study abroad. The smaller number of young people in the United States and other developed nations may require these countries to help their no-longer expanding workforce to become more productive. This development should further improve the position of women in both higher education and the economy, and it will press governments to enlarge the skills, education, and opportunities for their minority, immigrant, and perhaps their older citizens. Higher education and job training—and retraining—will be more important to ensure that the entire labor force is capable of productive work.

As birth rates decline and better nutrition, less arduous and dangerous work, and superior medical care keep persons alive longer, there will be an inexorable aging of the population in many countries. In the past thirty years China has added twenty-seven years to its citizens' average life expectancy. Life expectancy in Mexico is now around sixty-seven years, as high as it was in France in 1950. Chile and Singapore have joined the European nations with life expectancies of more than seventy years. In the United States the average life expectancy stands at seventy-eight years, compared with forty-eight years in 1900, and it is still rising. By the year 2030, the population of Americans over sixty-five years of age is predicted to double from 35.5 million persons in 2000 to roughly 70 million, and in 2030, the country will be home to more persons over sixty-five than under eighteen,[15] one-fifth of whom will be more than eighty-five years old.

This gerontological drift has already begun to have far-reaching consequences for every aging society and its educational expenditures. It also has begun to affect college and university programs, facilities, and pedagogy. The most profound consequence is for government budgets, which are becoming actuarially precarious as pension costs soar and health care spending continues to expand. At present, half of the U.S. federal domestic budget (excluding defense and interest on the federal debt) is spent on retired persons and the elderly, and more of each state's Medicaid monies every year go to nursing homes to care for the very old. The U.S. government now spends nine times as much per person on the elderly as it does on the young. Germany, Belgium, Sweden, and Japan have been forced to reform their pension systems, and the United States has decided to increase the retirement age for receiving full Social Security payments in tiny steps from sixty-five to sixty-seven between now and 2022 and to further increase Social Security taxes. Today, 70 percent of Americans pay more annually in Social Security taxes than they do in income taxes.

The elderly in the United States joined in 1958 to form the American Association of Retired Persons (AARP), an organization that now enrolls 33 million members (second in size in the nation only to the Roman Catholic Church) and employs fifteen full-time lobbyists and seventeen hundred employees.[16] Many older persons tend to vote against higher taxes, school bonds, and reductions in medical care, and they vote at a higher rate than do the young. What is less known is that America's elderly are the new rich, the healthiest, wealthiest old people in history. MIT management professor Lester Thurow argues that they are "a new class of people."[17] These "woopies" (well-off older people) have a median per capita income 67 percent above that of the population as a whole. As recently as 1970 the elderly were the poorest group in U.S. society, but today their poverty rate is lower and their median household wealth is greater than that of any other age group in the country. Increasingly, portions of the tuition of numerous college students are being paid by grandparents, especially through prepaid tuition plans and set-aside mutual funds.

The more alert colleges and universities have noticed this revolutionary shift in the numbers and fortunes of the elderly. Oberlin College has launched a Living and Learning Institute in Ohio, offering courses ranging from great literature to computer usage. The University of North Carolina at Asheville has established a College for Seniors, which includes a wellness program, a Research Institute to study issues of interest to seniors, and a retirement planning program. From Roger Williams University in Bristol, Rhode Island, to UCLA in Los Angeles, retirees can take special courses designed for them. Cornell University in Ithaca, New York, has helped start a retirement community in nearby Cayuga Heights, and Iowa State University helped build Green Hills, a university-affiliated retirement community for older alumni, faculty, and staff. Since 1980 Eckerd College in St. Petersburg, Florida, has run an Academy of Senior Professionals, who participate in the life and learning at the college. The late novelist James Michener and historian John Hope Franklin have been members. Hope College in Holland, Michigan, has a somewhat smaller but similar Academy for Senior Professionals. In 1988 Columbia University in New York City established the Society of Senior Scholars for thirty or so outstanding professors emeriti, who teach two courses a year to undergraduates and do research and writing.

In 1987, 3.1 percent of all enrolled undergraduate and 4.1 percent of all graduate students were more than fifty years old.[18] And these figures did not include the tens of thousands of older citizens taking one or two courses a year in continuing education programs. Nearly eighteen hundred institutions from the University of New Hampshire to New Mexico State University host participants in the Elderhostel Program. Elderhostel arranges for courses taught by scholars in classes lasting from five days to four weeks. The students are bands of fifty-five-and-older women and men, and the classes cover everything from archeology and Hispanic writers to local history and Japanese culture. In 2000 more than three hundred thousand older persons participated. There are also the Institutes for Lifelong Learning, where groups of retirees plan and run their own specially designed courses at community colleges like Edmonds Community College, north of Seattle, at small rural campuses like Young Harris College in north Georgia, or at major universities such as the University of Delaware.

The United States is hardly unique in responding to the explosive growth in educational interests among the elderly. Canada, Spain, Switzerland, and France also have academic programs for retirees. At the University of Toulouse in France, for instance, there is the Université du Troisième Age, with eight hundred or nine hundred elderly students a year studying such subjects as a foreign language, choral singing, art, finance, or physiology.

Changes in fertility and mortality, however, are not the only major demographic changes in American society. Two others—immigration and the metamorphosis of family life—are equally consequential for colleges and universities. In 1965, when the U.S. Congress was debating the Immigration and Nationality Act Amendments to abolish the preferences for immigrants from Europe, to increase immigration, and to stress family connections more than skills needed by the U.S. economy as criteria for entry, the bill's sponsor, Representative Emanuel Celler, a Democrat from Brooklyn, New York, assured everyone that the consequences of the bill would be "quite insignificant." In the Senate the bill's floor manager, Senator Edward Kennedy, a Democrat from Massachusetts, argued, "First, our cities will not be flooded with a million immigrants annually . . . Second, the ethnic mix of this country will not be upset."[19] The 1965 bill has resulted, however, in a dramatic transmogrification of the U.S. population. From 1965 to the present, America has absorbed more immigrants, illegal entrants, and aliens than all the other developed countries of the world combined. Some 37 million people, more than the population of Spain, South Korea, or Ireland, have entered.

About 1.2 million immigrants and refugees are being admitted legally each year, depending on world conditions and the number of those given political asylum, and the Immigration and Naturalization Service estimates that another seven hundred thousand or so may be annually entering the country illegally. This annual total is nearly five times as large as those admitted yearly before 1965, under the older, more discriminatory act. In addition, approximately three hundred thousand others enter the United States each year on student, work, or tourist visas and then frequently stay and never return to their homelands. The U.S. embassy in Beijing was ordered in 1996 to reduce the nonimmigrant visas granted to Chinese petitioners because the number of visas issued had quadrupled from 51,000 in 1990 to 200,000 in 1996, and each year one-fourth to one-third of the Chinese people with student, business, or tourist visas used them to relocate to America.

The ethnic makeup of U.S. immigrants since 1965 is very different from that in all previous periods. Before 1965 seven out of ten immigrants came from European countries and Canada. Since 1965 nearly nine in ten have come from Latin America and the Caribbean (48%–51%), from Asia (34%–36%), and from Africa (4%). In the 1980s alone, three Caribbean islands, for instance, were the source of roughly 10 percent of all immigrants: Dominican Republic, 251,803; Jamaica, 213,805; and Haiti, 140,163. And thousands more from these islands entered illegally. Los Angeles now has a "Little Saigon," a "Chinese Beverly Hills" in the Monterey Park area, and a "Koreatown." New York City's northern end of Manhattan is overwhelmingly populated with Dominicans, the Jackson Heights and Corona districts of the borough of Queens are filled with natives of Ecuador, and New York City is home to half the Chinese who entered illegally. St. Paul, Minnesota, and Wausau, Wisconsin, both have substantial numbers of Hmong people from the mountains of Laos, Vietnam, and Thailand. The Detroit metropolitan area has attracted considerable numbers of Muslims from the Middle East. More than a quarter million persons from the Philippines have migrated to California since 1965, and the greater Miami region of south Florida is crowded with Cuban émigrés. In New Jersey, Union City has become a Cuban enclave and Newark has a sizable Portuguese and Brazilian minority.

In the first decade of the twenty-first century, Hispanics will have surpassed blacks as the nation's largest minority. This is in large part the result of the huge influx of Mexicans and, more recently, persons from El Salvador, Honduras, and Nicaragua, a minority of whom are commuter migrants, unlike the earlier Irish, German, Sicilian, or Polish immigrants. In his outstanding book, *Strangers among Us: How Latino Immigration Is Trans-*

*forming America,* journalist Roberto Suro (the son of a Puerto Rican father and an Ecuadorian mother) writes:

> No other democracy has ever experienced an uninterrupted wave of migration that has lasted as long and has involved as many people as the recent movement of Spanish-speaking people to the United States. Twelve million foreign-born Latinos live here . . . The 6.7 million Mexican immigrants living in the United States in 1996 made up 27 percent of the entire foreign-born population, and they outnumbered the entire Asian immigrant population by more than 2 million people. . . .
>
> Latinos are different from all other immigrants past and present because they come from close by and because many come illegally . . . No immigrant group has carried the stigma of illegality that now attaches to many Latinos. . . .
>
> And the explosion does not involve just Mexicans now. The flows from Dominican Republic and El Salvador are also running at a rate headed for a doubling by the end of the decade. . . .
>
> The money sent home by Mexican workers in the United States totaled between \$2.5 and \$3.9 billion in 1995, according to estimates by a team of U.S. and Mexican scholars. At those levels, remittances equal about half the value of all foreign direct investment in [Mexico].[20]

For America's public schools, except those in states such as Wyoming, South Dakota, and Mississippi, this sustained and increasing immigration has presented a set of new problems. One person in nine over the age of five is now growing up in homes speaking a language other than English, according to a 2005 U.S. Census study. Thus, many elementary school teachers have to spend inordinate time just in teaching English. Numerous observers have also noted that the overall skill levels and education levels of many recent immigrants are considerably lower than those of immigrants prior to 1965. While a sizable minority of recent immigrants and illegal aliens are educated professionals, talented graduate students, and even Ph.D.'s—one-sixth of all U.S. physics teachers are estimated to be foreign-born, as are one in eleven female doctors—more than 43 percent of the immigrants (and a higher percentage of those who entered illegally) have not had a secondary school education. Moreover, the new immigrants possess various degrees of what the noted economist of immigration George Borjas calls "ethnic capital."[21]

Of course, America's colleges and universities have been altering their academic programs, faculty hiring, and campus activities to accommodate the tidal wave of immigrants. A majority of all institutions have launched major initiatives in "multiculturalism" or "diversity," novel programs such as Latino or Chicano Studies, new courses in comparative literature and religion and in the history of China, Japan, and sub-Saharan Africa, and new extracurricular political and social organizations. Intensive noncredit courses for English-as-a-Second Language have proliferated on numerous campuses from the Ivy League to the small Lutheran Concordia University in Portland, Oregon.

But some critics urge colleges to become more aggressive in recruiting immigrant youths and more receptive to them so that the future leadership in the United States will be close to representative of society's new demographic distribution.[22] This is comparatively easy to do for many Asian youths because of their often superior school records, but it is harder to do for the children, say, of Mexican immigrants because Mexican American students have the highest noncompletion rate from high school (almost 50%) of all ethnic groups. Yet the need for more education among young Mexican Americans is urgent because Mexican American women have the highest birth rate of any ethnic group, according to a 1998 National Center for Health Statistics report, and because the birth rate for Hispanic teenagers now exceeds that of black teenagers. Though Latinos have now become the largest U.S. minority group—36–38 million—they currently earn only 4 percent of the college degrees awarded.

There is another component of the new American society: the shifting forms of family life. The distinguished University of Pennsylvania demographer Samuel Preston recently wrote: "Perhaps the most significant social change of the past half century has been the reformation of the American family ... Americans are conducting an unprecedented social experiment with childhood, one with potentially profound effects on our nation's future."[23]

The radical change in American families has been the subject of dozens of recent books and articles by alert and diligent social scientists,[24] but many economists and policy analysts have been slow to include it as a major factor in their diagnoses, causing them to advocate faulty courses of action.[25] Among the more educated and politically liberal thinkers, personal behavior, the structure of families, morality, and character seem to have become subjects almost as taboo as sex was in the Victorian era.[26] Former Senator Daniel Patrick Moynihan has observed: "We have been defining deviancy down so as to exempt much conduct previously stigmatized, and also quietly raising the 'normal' level in categories where behavior [was] abnormal by any earlier standard."[27]

FIFTY YEARS AGO NEARLY 85 PERCENT of all U.S. children grew up in homes with a mother and a father, and a majority of mothers with children younger than puberty did not work or worked only part-time. Only 6 percent of the nation's children were born to unmarried women. Colleges and universities could usually count on a significant parental contribution toward tuition and on parental encouragement for students to be diligent in their studies.

But beginning in the 1960s the nuclear family began to crumble, and it crumbled with remarkable speed. Between 1960 and 2000 the divorce rate more than doubled, and the United States now has the highest divorce rate in the industrial world. The percentage of children born to unmarried women has jumped from 6 percent to 35 percent. Among blacks the percentage is now approaching 65 percent. But illegitimacy is increasing fastest among whites. The black out-of-wedlock rate was seven times higher than the white rate in 1970; it is now only 2.5 times higher. More than 63 percent of all out-of-wedlock births in the United States are now to white and Hispanic women. And numerous of these births are to teenage girls.

Though there has recently been a decline, nearly one million teen pregnancies occur in the United States each year, giving this country one of the highest teenage pregnancy rates in the developed world. About half of these pregnancies end in births. Many of the children born outside marriage grow up fatherless in single-parent households. About 27 percent of all U.S. children now live in single-parent households, and an estimated 60 percent of U.S. youngsters will spend a fraction of their youth with only one natural parent. Because of the spreading use of crack cocaine and other drugs, an estimated 8 percent of all U.S. children lose their young mothers, too, and have no parents at all. America faces a growing number of foster children and orphans—despite its position as the richest nation on earth. Married couples with children have declined to a mere 24 percent of all U.S. households. An estimated two million families with children are now headed by grandparents.

Moreover, the proportion of married mothers who have young children and are working full-time has climbed from 19 percent in the early 1960s to 70 percent in 2000, and the proportion of married women with children under one year of age and who return to work is approximately 53 percent.[28] So even where there is a two-parent household, more children are being raised with less parental time and attention.

The United States is not singular in this extraordinary development. Iceland, Sweden, and Denmark actually have a higher percentage of out-of-wedlock births, although more of these children are raised by two adults, and France, Britain, and Canada have comparable illegitimacy statistics. Princeton historian Lawrence Stone says: "The scale of marital breakdown in the West since 1960 has no historical precedent that I know of . . . There has been nothing like it in the last 2,000 years, and probably longer."[29]

Other prominent scholars have been struck by the collapse of traditional family structures and its consequences. For instance, Reynolds Farley, of the University of Michigan's Population Studies Center, believes that "the change in family is one of the most important social trends for American society in the past 30 years."[30] Still others are baffled by the way many policymakers and higher education executives disregard the startling change and, for the most part, express little concern about the development and its effects. Chester Finn Jr., the former assistant secretary for research and improvement in the U.S. Department of Education and a former professor of education at Vanderbilt, has written: "We know that a well-functioning society must condemn behavior that results in people having children who are not prepared to be good parents. I find it astonishing that . . . today we seem to attach more opprobrium to dropping out of school, experimenting on a cat, or uttering nasty remarks on campus than we do to giving birth to what, not so many years ago, were called 'illegitimate' children."[31]

The reasons for the sharp decline in traditional family life are numerous but somewhat mysterious. One could cite the change in values and personal behavior and the intensified individualism since the tumultuous 1960s;[32] the women's movement to be liberated from household chores, gain greater independence, and achieve full equality in the workplace; and the fact that most adolescents now reach puberty two years earlier than they did in 1900 and a year earlier than in the pre–World War II years.[33] The erosion of jobs in agriculture, mining, lumbering, construction, and manufacturing and the increase in the service sector have diminished the need for physical strength and created more work that women can perform equally well.[34]

Other contributing elements include the declining potency of religious proscriptions, the increasing display of sexual activity in films, television, and magazines, the expanded use of illicit drugs, the human potential movement among some psychologists that encourages adults to continue expending time and attention on their own growth more than on the growth of their children, and the contemporary focus of the federal government and the courts on individual rights (and the concomitant neglect of community needs and the mediating structures that Tocqueville found so estimable about the United States). And, of course, there is the expansion of the welfare state during the 1960s and 1970s, which increased state payments and subsidies to unwed mothers appreciably and neglected to hold unwed fathers responsible.

But whatever the reasons, the reformation of traditional family life is having profound effects on society, on children, and on schools and institutions of higher education. The most visible effect is the startling new poverty of the young. According to a 1998 study by the National Center for Children in Poverty, about 38 percent of the nation's poor today are children, who have replaced the elderly as the largest group in poverty. The center's director says that "the United States continues to have the highest rate of young-child poverty of any Western industrialized nation."[35] A major cause of this childhood poverty is the increase in numbers of children living with unmarried mothers. Such children are five times as likely to be poor as are those living with married parents. More than 60 percent of the households in the bottom quintile of family incomes are headed by women. Despite the considerable growth of the U.S. economy in the past forty years, the official poverty rate for children was roughly 150 percent higher in the later 1990s than in the early 1960s, when the so-called War on Poverty began at the federal level.

There were also four times as many persons serving time in prison in the mid-1990s than in the early 1960s, and 70 percent of all prison and reform school inmates come from fatherless families.[36] In her April 1993 *Atlantic Monthly* article, Barbara Defoe Whitehead wrote, "The relationship [between crime and single-parent families] is so strong that controlling for family configuration erases the relationship between race and crime and between low income and crime." Juvenile crime especially has exploded, along with other disorders of the young. According to the noted sociologist of family life, David Popenoe of Rutgers University:

> The collapse of children's well-being in the United States has reached breathtaking proportions. Juvenile violent crime has increased sixfold, from 16,000 arrests in 1960 to 96,000 in 1992, a period in which the total number of young people in the population remained relatively stable. Reports of child neglect and abuse have quintupled since 1976, when data were first collected. Eating disorders and rates of depression have soared among adolescent girls. Teen suicide has tripled. Alcohol and drug abuse among teenagers, although it has leveled off in recent years, continues at a very high rate.[37]

Young males, unattached to women and families, tend to be more aggressive, violent, prone to substance abuse, and disdainful of the rights of others. In a book exploring Gold Rush towns, cowboy life, hobo culture, juvenile drug distributors, crimes, and ghetto gangs, David Courtwright found that, whenever young men collect as singles without family influence, violent rowdiness often results.[38] Inner cities, where the percentage of out-of-wedlock births often approaches 80 percent, have sections like the male-dominated frontier towns of America's "wild" West. Daniel Patrick Moynihan once famously warned that a society full of unattached males "asks for and gets chaos."[39]

In sum, dissolution of the traditional family is a powerful factor in shaping what I believe is a qualitatively new society in the United States. The most authoritative review of the research on the consequences of single-parent families is the concise book *Growing Up with a Single Parent,* by Sara McLanahan of Princeton and Gary Sandefur of the University of Wisconsin, who

> reject the claim that children raised by only one parent do just as well as children raised by both parents . . . Compared with teenagers of similar background who grow up with both parents at home, adolescents who have lived apart from their parents during some period of childhood are twice as likely to drop out of high school, twice as likely to have a child before age 20, and one and a half times as likely to be "idle"—out of school and out of work—in their teens and early twenties. . . .
>
> Students in one-parent families have lower grades and poorer attendance records than children in two-parent families, even after test scores for aptitude are taken into account. [This] is troubling because it suggests that children from one-parent families are not as

motivated to work hard in school as children from two-parent families. Ability is important, but hard work and discipline are also essential for success.[40]

As for higher education, "The basic message is the same: family disruption continues to reduce children's school achievement after high school."[41] The research of Kathleen Kiernan of Britain's Family Policy Studies Centre and others confirms the findings of McLanahan and Sandefur. Young people, even those who are solidly middle class, are less likely to go to a university or to stay in, if accepted, when they come from divorced or single-parent families.[42] The evidence indicates that the two-parent or extended family may also be vital to what has come to be called student "self-esteem," the sense of self-worth, confidence, and personal capabilities necessary to deal with formal learning, relations with other persons, and life's complexities. One scholar notes that "we find it easier to love others if we ourselves have been loved. We learn self-sacrifice and commitment as we learn so many things—in small, manageable steps, starting close to home."[43]

In a fascinating study, Susan Mayer of the University of Chicago found that, contrary to platitudes about how the inequality of family income is the chief reason for the inequality of life outcomes, good parenting is more responsible than lack of cash. Children who are poor but whose parents and relatives teach them determination, diligence, healthy habits, and a respect for learning often do well in college, work, and life. "Once children's basic material needs are met, characteristics of their parents become more important to how they turn out than anything additional money can buy," Mayer says.[44] The brilliant achievements of many Jews from immigrant and impoverished families and, more recently, those of numerous Asians from similar economic backgrounds are testimony to Mayer's findings.

The family may be the most overlooked institution in U.S. policymaking and educational theories and practices. Until the past few decades, we usually took traditional families for granted and did not recognize sufficiently that many of the intellectual and artistic accomplishments in American life and much of the stature of our best colleges and universities are owed to families whose values, guidance, love, expectations, and devotion to education have produced young women and men who can handle and benefit from excellent academic training.

In several respects, it is mothers and fathers, not schools, who are the primary teachers of children, especially in the early formation of values, attitudes, behavior, and character. This was noted in the National Commission for Excellence in Education's 1983 report, *A Nation at Risk,* which emphasized that parents play the essential role in fostering children's inquisitiveness, self-confidence, discipline, and aspirations. Herbert Walberg found that the "curriculum of the home" is decisive because the first six years of life to a large extent determine a child's capacity for academic achievement later.[45] James S. Coleman called a two-parent family "the principal welfare institution in society."[46] It brings in and distributes income; provides housing, clothing, and emergency loans; and provides care when there is illness. Two-parent families also serve as a bank, a venture capital fund, a source of capital. Parents often make car payments and tuition payments for college, help their offspring start a business or buy a home, arrange for useful gifts at the time of a wedding and on birthdays, and, if possible, bestow an inheritance upon the parents' death. A young married couple with four parents and eight grandparents has a broad base of economic support and concern for the couple's future, a security network of kin. And two parents or an extended family are enormously helpful in teaching a child to read, prodding with homework, transporting the children, and talking about important current issues, moral dilemmas, and plans for the future.

A child without these benefits is clearly deprived and handicapped, as well as being, in many cases, poor. Woman-headed households are far more likely to be officially poor than are those headed by married couples. The U.S. Commission on Civil Rights contends that illegitimacy and divorce "are responsible for essentially all of the growth in poverty since 1970." And two policy analysts with the Progressive Policy Institute, the research arm of the Democratic Leadership Council, argue that "the best anti-poverty program for children is a stable, intact family."[47] Also, since children raised by single-parent families or divorced or foster parents are less likely to perform well in school, their shortcomings of formal education usually contribute to their poverty. In a 1995 report issued by the U.S. Census Bureau, 20.8 percent of those without high school diplomas were poor, while 9.3 percent of those who graduated from high school and only 5.5 percent of those who had one or more years of college were poor.[48] Despite arguments attributing other causes, poverty in contemporary society is often (though hardly exclusively) the result of broken and incomplete families and insufficient education.

Karl Marx predicted that under communism the state

would "wither away." Under advanced capitalism, however, the state has grown stronger and more intrusive, while the stable, two-parent family is the social institution that seems to be withering away. The consequences for America's youth and for colleges and universities are many.

The most easily quantifiable consequence for higher education is the increase in financial aid that colleges have had to supply. Even the richer private institutions today must return 20–25 percent of their tuition prices to many students partially because parental contributions have dwindled. In effect, most colleges and universities now receive only 70–75 percent of their "sticker price" of tuition. For independent colleges this is financially punishing, since tuition revenue composes roughly 55–65 percent of all revenues at private research universities, 65–70 percent at the stronger liberal arts colleges, and 70–80 percent at nonpublic comprehensive universities and underendowed small colleges. The amounts of financial aid have been especially large for the talented poor, especially black and Latino minority students, who are increasingly being raised in one-parent families. The federal government's Pell grants, introduced in 1972 as Basic Educational Opportunity Grants for the neediest undergraduates, have particularly been affected. In their study of financial aid, Michael McPherson and Morton Owen Schapiro found that "whereas in the early years of the program, most grant recipients were traditional-aged college students supported by their parents (in 1973–74 only 13 percent of Pell recipients were independent students), by 1985–86 the majority of recipients were independent students. The percentage has been fairly stable at around the 60 percent level during the 1990s." The phrase "independent students" is a euphemism for students who have a parent or parents who cannot (or will not) contribute to their child's college education. The two scholars also document that colleges and universities "have increased institutional financial aid at spectacular real rates."[49]

Another consequence of changing family life has been the extraordinary increase in the percentage of high school students, undergraduates, and graduate students who work part-time, or even full-time, while attending classes. To be sure, the students' desires to own their own stereo systems, automobiles, computer software, and elaborate clothing and the tripling of the real costs since 1960 of enrolling in colleges and universities have contributed to the increase. But for a growing number of young persons, their own employment has had to replace the previous sacrificial contributions of many two-parent households to their children's education. According to some estimates, two of every five high school seniors now work at least fifteen hours a week. Washington State has had to impose a twenty-hour limit on the work hours of sixteen- and seventeen-year-olds while school is in session, and a dozen other states have restricted the hours of work during school. Most colleges report that 60–70 percent of the students work twelve to twenty hours a week during the academic terms.[50] For graduate students, unless they attend a wealthy or generous university and receive a graduate fellowship, many are compelled to work nearly full-time during the years it takes to earn a doctoral degree.

The effects of work during college are mixed. Some claim it helps keep the work ethic strong among students and aids them in appreciating their subsidized higher education. Others complain that working students are often sleepy in class and inattentive and that they fail to complete their study assignments, tend to enroll in easier courses, and take five or six years to complete their undergraduate degrees or five to eight years to complete their doctoral degrees.

Moreover, the lack of a stable, strong, supportive two-parent family, or even a similar one-parent family,[51] is perhaps one reason that more undergraduates are involved in increased cheating, date-rapes, ethnic disparagements, and the growing celerity of students to accuse their professors of improprieties,[52] as well as having a self-pitying sense that they are "victims" of others who are somehow exploiting, ignoring, or demeaning them.[53] Values such as ethical behavior, fairness toward others, responsibility for one's own acts, and a deep respect for the enterprise of higher learning and its scholars are learned mostly at home, not in some brief orientation session for new undergraduates.

There is one other notable demographic change that has begun to have an influence on U.S. higher education. Young Americans are marrying or cohabiting with persons from other racial, ethnic, and religious groups in ever-increasing numbers. One observer calls it "the creolization of America"[54] and predicts that creoles will be the new majority of the population by the mid-twenty-first century. Between 1960 and 1990 interracial marriages increased more than 8 percent; in 1995, 8.4 percent of marriages (or one in twelve) were interracial.

The word *interracial* may not be an appropriate adjective, however. The Office of Management and Budget (OMB) 1977 Directive 15 decreed that there are four "racial" groups: whites, blacks, Asians and Pacific Islanders, and American Indians and Alaskan Natives. It also divides whites into Hispanic whites and non-Hispanic whites. But the Arab American Institute has objected that immigrants to the United States from the Middle East do not fit into any of the four categories. Many Asians object that to put Koreans, Filipinos, Pakistanis, and Chinese into the same demographic and racial category is absurd. Most Hispanics regard themselves principally as Puerto Ricans or Mexicans, Colombians or Cubans, Ecuadorians or Panamanians, not as "Hispanics," and many are mestizos who have some Indian, black, and European mixed ancestry. Many blacks in America also have a mixed ancestry. Booker T. Washington, Frederick Douglass, W. E. B. Du Bois, and Malcolm X, for example, had white as well as black forebears; Martin Luther King Jr. had an Irish grandmother and American Indian ancestry.[55] The emerging new prototypical American may be the young golfer Tiger Woods, who has black and Asian parents and white and American Indian forebears.

The data are clear. One-third of all young U.S.-born Hispanics are now intermarrying with Anglos.[56] About 36 percent of young native-born Asian men and 45 percent of young Asian women have married whites. An even larger percentage of American Indians, nearly one-half, have married whites. The number of black-white marriages has increased from 51,000 in 1960 to 311,000 in 1997. Half of all Italian Americans now marry non-Catholics, and nearly 40 percent of young American Jews have Gentile spouses.

Most colleges and universities still keep diversity statistics by the four OMB "racial" categories, and some institutions have affirmative action goals by "race." But racial, ethnic, and religious intermarriages are beginning to produce freshmen who do not fit neatly into any category. It is no wonder that the idea of affirmative action in its present form is increasingly viewed as outmoded, although there is still considerable support on most campuses for special treatment of nonimmigrant African Americans, most of whose ancestors cruelly suffered from slavery and until recently from widespread discrimination. The growing creolization of the students, staff, and faculty in U.S. higher education could diminish the current high degree of attention to racial, ethnic, and religious classifications.

## Technology

Another development is contributing to the creation of a substantially new society in the United States: the revolution in communication. Since higher education is an enterprise that in essence communicates the best ideas, art, skills, processes, and accounts of life from learned elders to young learners and that communicates its new findings among scholars worldwide, this revolution is both galvanizing and upsetting for colleges and universities. Indeed, a few digital evangelists and rabid futurists have prophesied that traditional college campuses and scholarly journals may not be needed in several decades.

Just as trains and fast ships and then automobiles and airplanes enabled the development of national economies and international trade, suburban housing, faster mail, increased travel, and universities with a national representation of students,[57] so the accumulation of novel communication vehicles—cell phones, films, audio and video cassettes, computers, facsimile machines, satellites, iPods, the Internet, tapes and compact discs, computer networks, CD-ROMs, Web pages—is leading to radical new ways to gather and exchange information internationally. The transformation is deepened by new combinations of communications media such as telecommunications and teleprocessing or television and satellites. The wrench for American society is phenomenal.

Whole industries, such as steelmaking, have been diminished or changed, as have the telephone companies, and thousands of new companies have sprung up to handle the burgeoning of the new communication technology, including adolescent giants such as Google, Intel, Microsoft, and Cisco Systems. Optical fibers are replacing copper wires, and such new fields as materials science and software engineering have been born. Individuals obtain information in new, faster ways and link with persons who have similar interests elsewhere in the nation and in distant corners of the world. Architects design buildings and engineers design products on a screen instead of on paper, and doctors diagnose differently. Mail is increasingly sent via e-mail or facsimile machines and delivered in minutes instead of days. Books can be searched for and purchased via computer without leaving one's office or home. Many factory workers are being retrained as "knowledge workers," and new management styles have had to be introduced.[58] Numerous organizations are being "re-engineered."[59]

The latest communication revolution is actually the third that people have had to confront. The first was writing, which probably began in hieroglyphic form in Egypt about 3200 BCE and in cuneiform with the Sumerians in Mesopotamia (southern Iraq) around 3000 BCE.[60] When the traders of northern Egypt, Phoenicia (present-day Lebanon), and Syria conceived of the alphabet and developed the first script around 1500 BCE, writing among the Semites, Egyptians, and Greeks gradually spread in use, enabling the recording of such works as the Old Testament and the epic stories of Homer.

We may not think of writing as a technology but it is. It requires that people construct and invent writing tools (reeds, feather quills, brushes, chalk, pencils,[61] stones that mark), writing surfaces (animal skins, papyrus, cloth, slates, paper), and inks, juices, or paints. For the cultural evolution of humankind, writing may be the most important technology ever developed. In his classic work Walter Ong expressed that view: "Writing is in a way the most drastic of the three technologies. It initiated what print and computers only continue, the reduction of dynamic sound to quiescent space, the separation of the word from the living present, where alone spoken words can exist. By contrast with natural oral speech, writing is completely artificial. There is no way to write 'naturally.'"[62]

Writing ushered in a wholly new way to think, to live. It moved humans away from an exclusively aural-oral mode of jaw-to-jaw communication to a complementary new sensory world of visual communication. It reduced the need for memorization, proverbs, stories, and aural aides like rhymes and repetitions, and it increased internal consciousness and scrutiny at a slight distance from the natural world and human behavior. It enabled people to compile historical texts, as Herodotus and Thucydides did. It gave rise to libraries[63] and to individualism, too, because while oral communication is often a group activity, writing and reading are usually solitary. It reduced the power of the tribe's elders and priests. With the introduction of numerical writing and symbols, people could also exchange mathematical ideas and calculations for the first time. Ong claims that "writing . . . was and is the most momentous of all human technological inventions."[64] It changed cultural life on this planet forever.

The second technological revolution was the introduction of printing in the mid-fifteenth century by Laurens Koster of Holland, Pamfilo Castaldi of Italy, and Johann Gutenberg of Germany. Printing was facilitated by the previous invention of paper manufacturing in thirteenth-century Europe for use by the clergy, merchants, and political rulers. Unlike the technology of writing, which took centuries to be accepted (and is still not in use in some remote tribal cultures), the technique of engraved movable type pressed into paper spread with remarkable speed throughout Europe. One scholar found that, "unknown anywhere in Europe before the mid-fifteenth century, printers' workshops would be found in every important municipal center by 1500. They added a new element to urban culture in hundreds of towns."[65]

Like writing, the new technology of printing was revolutionary in its repercussions. It gave birth to the art of engraving and the introduction of artists' prints, and it prompted the opening of new universities. It changed pedagogy from an almost entirely oral style of teaching, as Abelard and others practiced it, to one of lectures plus readings. "Mechanick printers" enabled the Protestant Reformation and family Bible reading at home. They allowed mariners and explorers to have printed maps, speeded the exchange of new mathematical, scientific, and political ideas, and brought the texts of Aristotle, Thomas Aquinas, and Euclid to a larger number of readers. Libraries sprouted. So did music and book publishers. Gradually scholars and lawyers abandoned much of their heavily argumentative and rhetorical style for a more bookish, evidential approach. Brilliant, showy lectures gave way to pedantry, although oral examinations still remain at numerous universities as part of the doctor of philosophy examination.

Now digital electronics is recasting economic and cultural life again. And computers and the other new technologies surrounding them are rapidly transforming research, teaching, and exchanges in higher education. Unlike the changes brought on by printing, the innovations in electronic communication have entered our lives with astonishing speed. After the transistor was developed in 1948, the use of silicon was greatly expanded in the mid-1950s, and the integrated circuit was invented in 1957, there has been a rush of other new elements.

| early 1960s | mainframe computer |
| 1971 | microprocessor |
| early 1970s | optical fibers |
| 1977 | Apple II |
| 1981 | IBM PC |
| early 1980s | Internet |
| mid-1980s | facsimile machines |
| 1984 | mouse; cellular telephone |
| 1990 | World Wide Web |
| early 1990s | networks |
| 1992 | Windows |
| 1994 | browser |
| 1998 | Google |

Thus, in the past half century, and especially in the past twenty-five years, a wholly new communications network has burst into being. We are rapidly moving from a world of words to one of bits. A bit, says Nicholas Negroponte of MIT's Media Lab, is a 1 or a 0 that "has no color, size, weight, and it can travel at the speed of light." There are also bits that tell us about other bits. Both travel at 6 million bits per second over the more than $60 billion worth of telephone lines installed throughout the United States. And, says Negroponte, "These two phenomena, commingled bits and bit-about-bits, change the media landscape so thoroughly that concepts like video-on-demand and shipping electronic games down your local cable are just trivial applications—the tip of a much more profound iceberg."[66]

The enabling mechanism and facilitator of bit exchanges and calculations is the Internet, a fabric of fifty thousand or so networks, with millions of host processors, that can send messages around the globe or to any professor's home computer screen in seconds. Retired IBM executive Leslie Simon observed that "the Internet can take the place of a post office, a telephone, a broadcast studio, an insurance agent, a sound recording studio, a movie theater, an automobile dealership . . . The medium is no longer the message. In cyberspace, media can take any form—video, print, graphics, or sound—at the whim of the user." Traffic on the Internet is estimated to be doubling every one hundred days or so. In 1997 there were roughly 2.7 trillion e-mail messages, "many times more than the amount of mail delivered by the world's post office."[67]

For higher education, the rapid introduction of computers, the Internet, and the World Wide Web has had major consequences. Exactly how profound the consequences will be and how colleges and universities will eventually respond to the new mode of digital, global communication are unclear. Some enthusiasts have proclaimed that "the invention of the computer is one of the pivotal events in the history of civilization" and that its full use "will mark the beginning of the next level of civilization."[68] Less fervent analysts, such as media theorist John Thompson, recognize that the development of new networks of communication and information flow helps create "new forms of action and interaction in the social world, new kinds of social relationships, and new ways of relating to others and to oneself." But he adds that, "for all the talk of postmodernism and postmodernity, there are precious few signs that the inhabitants of the late twentieth century world have recently entered a new age."[69]

Whether the prophets of a new cyber age or the skeptics who recall other major technological advances and remember earlier pronouncements (such as the 1957 Ford Foundation report that predicted that television would be "the greatest opportunity for the advancement of education since the introduction of printing by moveable type") are more reliable remains to be seen. The world of higher learning has already benefited greatly, especially in its research, from computers and is likely to require some restructuring because of the new communication technology. The inescapable fact is that computers provide students with an alternative way of gathering information, calculating, and learning and give professors enhanced methods of teaching.

In one of the more thoughtful books on the subject, Jay David Bolter predicts that more of tomorrow's writing and reading will be distributed in electronic form:

The printed book, therefore, seems destined to move to the margin of our literate culture. The issue is not whether print technology will completely disappear; books may long continue to be printed for certain kinds of texts and for luxury consumption. But the idea and the ideal of the book will change. Print will no longer define the organization and presentation of knowledge ... Electronic technology offers us a new kind of book and new ways to write and read. The shift to the computer will make writing more flexible, but it will also threaten the definitions of good writing and careful reading that have been fostered by the technique of printing.[70]

As for teaching, here is how another scholar portrays some current teaching at her university:

An aeronautical engineering professor is lecturing to her class on wing design when interactive video enables a classmate from one of several remote company sites to interrupt and explain that his company's wing design practice is now different. Interactive video links students in three locations to a music class; a third of the class is on campus, a third is at San Jose State University, and a third is at Princeton University. Together the class critiques a classical performance. In another classroom, only a fourth of the students enrolled in the class are present for a physics lecture; the remainder had schedule conflicts and will watch the lecture later, on video, by logging on to the World Wide Web.[71]

The library, usually the center of a college or university campus, especially in twentieth-century academic life, has presented a major quandary. Campus libraries have been adding computer labs, music and video listening rooms, photocopiers, cybercafes, video viewing rooms, and group discussion areas alongside traditional individual study carrels. They have joined collaborative networks, collected CD-ROMs, and put their card catalogs on line. They have added information desks to assist students and faculty in accessing data sources. And the long-held view that a campus library's greatness is measured by the numbers of books it contains and journals it subscribes to is being reassessed. What to do with print-oriented campus libraries has become a huge and increasingly expensive vexation. Two of America's experts express the dilemma neatly:

> Traditional notions of libraries and information technology organizations are no longer intellectually and economically sustainable. Digitally produced volumes of paper publications rendered obsolete the concept of self-sufficient collections. [Yet] linear planning strategies, so well adapted to the characteristics of print-on-paper, are useless in predicting the course and cost of digital technology. We must adopt an exceedingly agile approach, capable of balancing a variety of beginnings. . . .
>
> There are no solutions to these problems within the traditional organizational structures. We must reconceive the overall information and service strategies of our campus in a manner that incorporates continuous change as a way of life and is unconstrained by the historical legacies of institutional organization.[72]

Clearly, the introduction of new communication technologies has prompted substantial changes and contributed to both the substance of a new kind of society and novel practices and conundrums in higher education.

## Economics

A third development that has helped to shape a considerably new society since the 1970s is the set of changes in America's economy. The changes are major, structural, and of great consequence to the nation's colleges and universities, especially when combined with new demographics, technologies, and sociopolitical convictions.

The growth of America's economy in recent decades is a chronicle of astonishing success. But the chronicle has two parts. One is the period from the end of World War II until the mid-1970s; the other part is the transformative period from the 1970s to the present. Both periods have had fundamental effects on U.S. higher education.

Except for most older Americans, it is difficult to imagine what the country was like in the 1940s. Nearly one-fourth of the population still lived on farms, of which only one-third had electricity and one-tenth had flush toilets. Of U.S. houses in the mid-1940s, 30 percent had no running water, 58 percent had no central heat, and 80 percent were heated by wood or coal. Half did not have electric refrigerators, and one in seven did not even have a radio. Families ate half as much meat and poultry as we do today, and many cooked with lard. More than 90 percent of all black persons lived in rural areas, many in extreme poverty, and they were excluded from many kinds of employment, major sports teams, and most colleges. The infant mortality rate was four times as high as it is today. Half the labor force had arduous jobs in factories and mines, on farms and fishing boats, and in such fields as construction or lumbering. Sixty percent of adults described themselves as working class, and only one-third viewed themselves as middle class.[73]

Not surprisingly, in the 1940s only one in four adults had earned a high school diploma and less than 4 percent of all adults had completed college. Many people in the United States were relatively poor, especially since the nation was still climbing out of a grievous economic depression; most were culturally unsophisticated and uneducated, at least through formal schooling.

But World War II had left America's land unscathed, unlike that of the country's major competitors, who had suffered heavy wartime damage to their facilities, finances, and male workforce. Americans seized this opportunity with aggressive enterprise and created the world's mightiest economy. MIT economist Frank Levy reports that, "The entire period from 1947 to 1973 was a 27–year boom."[74] By 1960 the United States was producing half the world's output, and by 1970 U.S. family incomes had increased by 60 percent and the proportion of people in poverty had declined from 22 percent to 12 percent. Between 1945 and 1961, the nation experienced the greatest explosion in births in U.S. history, the so-called baby boom.

Jobs in manufacturing increased, and in the 1950s alone the number of those who worked on farms dropped from seven to four million. The number of owner-occupied homes doubled, and the number of automobiles and trucks quintupled. Many African Americans left the South to migrate to big northern cities. By 1970, a majority of U.S. citizens saw themselves as middle class.

HIGHER EDUCATION AND THE NEW SOCIETY

The federal government, flush with tax dollars, compassionate liberals, and economic optimism, initiated in the 1960s a bundle of expensive new programs: Medicare, an overhaul of the immigration laws, Medicaid, food stamps, and a sizable increase in the monies for Aid to Families with Dependent Children (AFDC). In 1965, President Lyndon Johnson signed the Higher Education Act, increasing the opportunity for more students to attend college. Later, in 1972, Congress approved the Basic Education Opportunity Grants for low-income students. Between 1963–64 and 1975–76, federal aid to higher education students soared from $1.1 million to $23.2 million.[75]

Federal aid for America's needy, including needy college students, was only one of the national government's historic changes of the 1960s. The other was the massive increase in funding for scientific research and development. Stimulated initially by World War II and Vannevar Bush's 1945 report, *Science, the Endless Frontier*, then shocked by the Soviet Union's launch of the space satellite Sputnik in 1957, federal officials poured unprecedented millions of dollars into engineering and scientific research and development (R&D). Leaders also decided that the universities, not corporations, should receive nearly all the money for basic research. As one scholar of education wrote: "[By the early 1970s] the 400–odd separate programs through which Washington channeled money into higher education . . . were administered by 25 separate federal agencies and more than 50 major organizational units within those agencies."[76]

Two other historians declared, "The post-Sputnik surge of federal research funding had indisputably inaugurated a golden age for academic science,"[77] especially at the top thirty or so finest research universities. Between 1963 and 1976, federal R&D funds for these universities rose from $830 million to $2.4 billion, a 300 percent increase. President Lyndon Johnson's "Great Society" legislation in 1965 even established a National Endowment for the Humanities and a National Endowment for the Arts and provided some research dollars for social scientists as well, though foundations continued to be the chief supporters of social and historical research.

One of the most penetrating of the analyses of U.S. higher education during the decade was that of Clark Kerr. In his 1963 Godkin Lectures at Harvard, Kerr wrote that America's leading research universities were becoming "federal grant universities." As Kerr viewed the development of the early 1960s, the research-oriented universities were increasingly being regarded as a novel kind of dynamo for the nation's economy, military, and culture: "The university today finds itself in a quite novel position in society . . . The basic reality . . . is the widespread recognition that new knowledge is the most important factor in economic and social growth . . . The university has become a prime instrument of national purpose. This is new."[78]

It was not only the research universities that benefited from the largesse of the 1960s. With enrollments increasing, especially among women and foreign students, and with monies for new construction and higher faculty salaries, many of the other three thousand or so colleges and universities also began to enlarge and partially transform themselves. To later commentators, despite the disruptive student protests and vandalism of 1968–71, the 1960s seem to many a "golden age."[79]

The 1970s, however, were a different story. In fact, it was a decade that, to a considerable extent, ushered in a relatively new America. As one scholarly chronicle contended: "The Seventies transformed American economic and cultural life . . . In race relations, religion, family life, politics, and popular culture the 1970s marked the most significant watershed of modern U.S. history, the beginning of our own time."[80] Another observer is convinced that the 1970s produced "the most total transformation that the United States has lived through since the coming of industrialism."[81] These two appraisers are not alone. The remarkable economic boom of the post–World War II years eroded in the 1970s and then collapsed and had to be rebuilt. And in response U.S. higher education was pressed to make numerous changes, a few of them fundamental. The economic decline of the 1970s was the worst since the depression of the 1930s.

The assault on the U.S. economy was double-barreled, coming from both external and internal sources. Well-made goods, especially from Japan and Germany, began entering the United States, and in 1971, for the first time in the twentieth century, the nation imported more goods than it exported. In 1970, imports into the country totaled around $40 billion, but by 1980 they had climbed to $245 billion. By 1980, one-fourth of all manufactured goods sold in America were made abroad. Economists and business and government leaders, used to thinking of the U.S. economy as a largely self-contained system, had to begin thinking more adroitly about an internationally competitive economy and foreign markets, while at the same time improving their environmental discharges because Congress created the Clean Air Act of 1970, the Environmental Protection Agency, and the Toxic Substances Control Act of 1976.

A second external assault was the outbreak of terrorism around the world. Between 1968 and 1981, terrorists and assassins murdered the American ambassadors to Cyprus, Guatemala, Lebanon, and Sudan and also the president of Egypt, the prime ministers of Jordan and Spain, the Queen of England's uncle, and nearly the Pope. The Irish Republican Army murdered more than twenty-two hundred people and planted seventy-five hundred bombs, killing six hundred people and maiming more than one thousand others. Palestinian terrorists attacked the Munich Olympics in 1972 and killed eleven Israeli athletes, and in 1976 German and Arab terrorists hijacked an Air France jetliner and flew it to Uganda's Entebbe Airport, where the hostages were rescued in a daring midnight raid by Israeli commandos.[82] The terrorism continues to this day and remains a growing expense for the United States.

Terrorism has created an increasing financial problem for the national, state, and major municipal economies, each of which has had to increase security procedures, especially against the persistent threats from Muslim radical extremists. The United States has been compelled to establish a costly new Department of Homeland Security.

A third external disturbance was the rise in inflation from 1970 to 1983, the worst in peacetime in the twentieth century. The Vietnam War brought enlarged deficits to the federal budget. Then in October 1973, Egypt and Syria invaded Israel, only to be quickly driven back in the so-called Yom Kippur War. In retaliation, the OPEC countries reduced output and raised their oil prices 300 percent, causing long lines at gasoline stations. At the same time, the Soviets had a crop failure and other countries had food shortages, so between 1972 and 1974, U.S. food prices rose 34 percent. By 1974, inflation had reached 11 percent, and the median family income started falling. In 1979, the Shah of Iran was overthrown and oil prices rose another 300 percent. President Carter, attempting to reduce inflation, appointed Paul Volcker as chief of the Federal Reserve Board in July 1979. Volcker applied stern measures and reduced inflation from 12–13 percent in 1979 to 3.8 percent in 1983 but not without inflicting a recession in 1982–83. Mortgage rates rose to 12 percent. Debt for both individuals and corporations skyrocketed. Historian James Patterson claims that "the mood of the late 1970s was in important ways the gloomiest in late twentieth-century history."[83]

In addition to external factors, the United States contributed to the economic malaise of the 1970s with internal blunders, lapses, and failures to respond to the rapidly changing economic situation. Many state, city, and federal government leaders seemed unable to rein in their prodigal expenditures of the 1960s and instead just kept raising taxes. The percentage of federal income taxes paid by the average family doubled in the 1970s, and the contribution required for Social Security increased from 9.6 percent in 1970 to 13.2 percent in 1981. Property and sales taxes also escalated. Welfare caseloads exploded, with fifteen million Americans on public assistance by the late 1970s and twenty-one million persons on food stamps. Numerous cities such as Cleveland, Detroit, and New York City approached bankruptcy, and several states like California could not halt their prodigal spending habits, prompting tax revolts. American trade unions demanded huge wage and benefit increases, and steelworkers, truck drivers, and railroad workers, among others, received more than 30 percent increases over three years. In 1978, according to the Bureau of Labor Statistics, the average earnings of U.S. automobile workers were 12 percent higher than those of America's college professors.

Another internal cause of the economic downturn was the rending of the nation's social fabric. Beginning in the late 1960s, the crime rate in the United States increased enormously; and during the 1970s, robberies, assaults, rapes, larcenies, auto thefts, and murders all increased. Homicides among young males increased by 45 percent, often connected with battles over illegal drugs. The 1970s was also the decade of increased cocaine use, even in factories, schools and colleges, and Wall Street offices. The decade was one of sexual revolt and experimentation, too. Books such as Erica Jong's *Fear of Flying* and Alex Comfort's *Joy of Sex* became best sellers. The number of divorces increased from 650,000 in 1970 to more than 1 million annually, giving America the highest divorce rate in the developed world.[84] The Catholic Church, opposed to divorce, increased the number of annulments seventy-seven-fold between 1969 and 1981.[85] U.S. teenage pregnancy and abortion rates also skyrocketed to the highest in the developed world, and in 1973 the U.S. Supreme Court decided the famous *Roe v. Wade* case.

The radical change in family life meant that one American youngster in three, and nearly three in four black children, were suddenly growing up in one-parent households, and children replaced the elderly as the largest poverty group in the land. This development brought on major changes, not only in social welfare payments but also in the educational, social, and financial abilities of America's youth.

The 1970s were called the "me decade,"[86] a new age when play and leisure were predicted to replace the work ethic, and personal growth, satisfaction, and "liberation" would become central. Adults young and old began jogging, bicycling, switching to health foods, joining encounter groups, flocking to rock music concerts, or trying new religious experiences that more closely suited their own inner needs. As one of the young rebels, Jerry Rubin, confessed in 1976, "In five years, from 1971 to 1975, I directly experienced est, Gestalt therapy, bioenergetics, rolfing, massage, jogging, health foods, tai chi, Esalen, hypnotism, modern dance, meditation, Silva Mind Control, Arica, acupuncture, sex therapy, Reichian therapy, and More House."[87] The social historian Christopher Lasch, possibly the most perspicacious analyst of the period, concluded that, "in a dying culture, narcissism appears to embody—in the guise of personal 'growth' and 'awareness'—the highest attainment of spiritual enlightenment."[88]

Internally, the 1970s were also years of political weakness and tumult. In 1973, President Richard Nixon and his aides were caught trying to cover up a break-in of the Democratic Party offices at the Watergate Apartments, prompting Nixon to resign the presidency in 1974. This shocking executive branch affair seemed to cause much of the media to become more adversarial, even hostile, to public figures and policies and negative about social developments generally. As one scholarly journalist recently wrote, "Highly speculative bad news is often given considerable play by the United States media, while confirmed good news is barely reported . . . Western life is methodically made to sound perilous or precarious by media spin."[89]

Nixon's replacement, Gerald Ford, was ineffective and devoid of leadership skills, and the new president elected in 1976, Jimmy Carter, a spiritual and well-intentioned man, turned out to be reluctant to work with Congress, unable to delegate, and unsophisticated. Polls revealed among the public a widespread new contempt for authority.

President Carter, incidentally, the former governor of Georgia, was indicative of the extraordinary shift of American politics to the southern tier of the country. Except for the interregnum presidency of Gerald Ford in 1974 to 1976, no American president since Lyndon Johnson assumed the office in 1963 has come from outside the South, that sunny section from Georgia to southern California. And with the shift has come a growing prominence of southern culture: conservative religion and televangelists, NASCAR racing, the decline of trade unions, Elvis Presley, Garth Brooks, and the rediscovery of country music, pick-up trucks, and cowboy boots. In the 1970s and 1980s, half of the annual foreign investment in the United States went to the states below the Mason-Dixon line.

In addition, the 1970s experienced a rise in the arguments over affirmative action policies. Numerous colleges, universities, and government agencies, in order to increase the number of minority students, had begun enrolling African Americans with what were seen as low credentials, often employing quotas. The situation came to a head when a white, highly qualified student, Allan

Bakke, applied in 1973 to the medical school of the University of California at Davis, a school that had reserved 16 percent of its entering class for minority students. He was rejected. Noting that many of the minority students had lower grade point averages and test scores, Bakke appealed and then sued in a case that reached the U.S. Supreme Court in 1977. By a five-to-four decision, the court in 1978 ruled that Allan Bakke had been wrongfully denied admission. The swing vote was given by Justice Lewis Powell, who argued that universities could not admit or exclude persons solely on the basis of race but could consider color and ethnicity as one factor in building a more diverse class. Soon many institutions began seeking more African Americans, Hispanics, Asians, and women, and the diversity movement in America was launched.[90]

The economic downturn of the 1970s also prompted considerable rethinking and ushered in several profound structural changes in U.S. capitalism and economic practices. These alterations brought numerous consequences to America's colleges and universities.

Capitalism, which largely benefited the capitalists, transformed itself into a worldwide market economy, increasingly benefiting consumers through new products and services, cheaper goods from abroad, and often goods of higher quality. A decline in government regulation over industries hastened the change. Two scholars of international economics noted that, "As late as 1970, imports into the U.S. totaled only $40 billion; by 1980, they had climbed to $245 billion and by 1984, to almost $350 billion . . . Once American firms dominated world markets; now they must adjust to them . . . We are . . . in the midst of a major industrial transition."[91] The proportion of international trade since 1970 has increased roughly thirteenfold and now accounts for nearly 24 percent of America's gross domestic product. There is a new international division of labor. But the emphasis on "globalization" should not be overdone; as one economist observed, "We are still a long way from a single world market."[92]

The metamorphosis to a more global economy meant that the United States increasingly farmed out lower-skill manufacturing to nations with an abundance of lower labor costs while concentrating more heavily on new technology, fundamental scientific inquiries, inventions, international trade, innovative marketing and retailing, and other fields where American individualism and entrepreneurial vigor provided a comparative advantage. Daniel Bell, one of the most insightful social theorists of the late twentieth century, wrote that "a major feature of a post industrial society is the rise of science-based industries—polymers, optics, electronics, telecommunications—that derive from the codification of theoretical knowledge."[93]

The shift from a mainly domestic capitalism to a far more international market economy, aided by the rise of new technology, caused profound changes throughout America's social order. For one vital thing, it heightened the validity of contentions by economists such as Jacob Mincer, Theodore Schultz, and Gary Becker that human capital—the quality of a nation's workforce—is the most valuable asset for the emerging economy. The United States needed smarter, more internationally attuned, and more scientifically educated persons in its workforce if the country was to preserve its prosperity.

In the 1970s, therefore, more persons—young, older,

female, blacks, even blue-collar workers—rushed to increase their knowledge and skills. Junior colleges became public two-year community colleges, of which there were 1,049 by 1980–81, and more of those students were transferring to four-year institutions or preparing for more complicated technical work because the revolution in science and technology altered the nature of vocational work. As two scholars described the changes,

> Scientific specialization encourages the proliferation of secondary support occupations . . . Like engineering, technicians' work blurs the boundary between mental and manual work, and by extension, between blue- and white-collar labor. Technicians often wear white collars, carry briefcases, and conduct sophisticated scientific and mathematical analyses. Yet they use tools and instruments, work with their hands, create objects, repair equipment, and, from time to time, get dirty.[94]

A new category of workers, similar to professionals in some ways but also similar to craftspeople, came into being.

The metamorphosis of the economy also resulted in the decline of the number of workers belonging to trade unions, a number that peaked in 1978. It prompted many large corporations to reduce the number of their employees and prompted a large increase of new, smaller firms of fifty to four hundred workers and of nonprofit service entities. The change inverted the hours that different groups of people worked. The new entrepreneurs, professionals (including the more productive professors), and the growing number of advanced technicians were working fifty to sixty hours a week while many in trade unions and routine jobs labored only forty hours or less. Economist Robert William Fogel found that, "Between the late 1960s and the late 1980s, the hours worked by industrial professionals and highly skilled technicians who dominate the highest income decile increased by 12 percent. By contrast, the hours worked in the poorest decile declined by 20 percent."[95] The need to create a more market-oriented and international economy gave rise to a growing number of strategists and future-minded managers and consultants, as well as talk of "reengineering" companies for the emerging global economy.[96] Unfortunately, the need to confront novel conditions also contributed to a decline in the illuminating study of history, as historian J. H. Plumb observed: "Industrial society . . . does not need the past. Its intellectual orientation is towards change rather than conservation, towards exploitation and consumption. The new methods, new processes, new forms of living of scientific and industrial society have no sanction in the past and no roots in it."[97]

The 1970s, however, were not only years of deterioration and disruptive change for the U.S. economy. The decade was also one in which there were numerous achievements, innovations, and the birth of wholly new industries. The 1970s saw the introduction of microwave ovens, the Sony Walkman, pocket calculators, fiberoptic technology, seat belts for automobile drivers, the Apple computer, and Microsoft software. The decade saw the birth of transforming new companies such as Federal Express, Wal-Mart, and Intel. In 1976, the United States celebrated its bicentennial and Americans won five Nobel Prizes. Cooking and nutrition improved, and an enlarged U.S. wine industry blossomed. Women in

1972 received equality in college athletics from Title IX, and generally were being selected more frequently for important positions, as were educated African Americans.

Beginning in the 1970s, but from 1983 to the present, the American economy transformed itself into what has been dubbed an "information economy" or a "knowledge economy," especially after the introduction of the World Wide Web in 1990–91, the browser in 1993–94, and search engines like Google in 1998–99. During the 1990s, the U.S. economy spurted ahead of the other leading economies. Historian Philip Jenkins claimed in 2006, "In November 1982, the U.S. economy began one of its longest and most triumphant periods of growth and expansion, a trend scarcely broken until 2000."[98] Productivity in America was the world's highest; inflation remained low; unemployment dropped below 5 percent; and median family income increased. Manufacturing, despite outsourcing, remained strong, requiring fewer workers because of new capital investments and the nation's highly efficient workers. The United States exported aerospace equipment, pharmaceuticals, computer chips and software, movies, insurance, banking, consulting, and more. The stock market, which topped 2,000 in the Dow Jones index in 1987 for the first time, rocketed to over 11,500 in 2000 and higher still in 2006. An estimated two-thirds of all adult U.S. citizens now own stock, either personally or through their IRAs, 401(k) accounts, or other retirement plans. In addition, smog in America declined by one-third between 1980 and 2005, and many of the nation's corporations became more energy efficient.

American exports have risen nearly 9 percent a year since 1985. International trade now accounts for 24 percent of the U.S. gross national product, a huge increase over that of 1983.[99] The much lamented U.S. trade deficit includes only goods traded, ignoring the service sector, which now employs 70 percent of America's workforce. In the new global economy, the United States has performed admirably. More wealth has been created in America since 1983 than in the previous 150 years.

As one would expect, the country's new economy since the 1970s has brought into being a cluster of changes in business and in society. Large corporations employ fewer workers and sell more outside the United States. New firms have sprung up, and research and innovations have increased. The Bayh-Dole Act of 1980 allowed academic institutions to create products based on patents developed in their research and encouraged industries and universities to work more closely together. The measure also stimulated the growth of research parks near academic institutions and led numerous professors to form or participate in new companies.[100]

But the most widely discussed consequence of the new economy has been the formation of a new socioeconomic class structure among America's population, often referred to as the problem of the increasing inequality of wealth. The data reveal that there are more wealthy persons than ever in the United States, that the middle class has been shrinking, and that real wages for blue-collar and most service workers have remained relatively stable. In effect, the burgeoning economic growth since the early 1980s has altered the distribution of earnings and wealth in the nation. How and why has this happened?

The blossoming U.S. economy of the past two decades has required more scientists, engineers, bold innovators, greater cultural achievements, more internationally attuned persons, and smarter, more competitive young people. As Michael Young predicted in his remarkably percipient 1959 book, "To withstand international competition the country had to make better use of its human material . . . The needs of the economy reshaped society."[101] Or, as economist Finis Welch wrote, "The root cause underlying the growth in wage inequality in the United States has been growth in the demand for 'skill,' broadly defined."[102] Suddenly, those with advanced skills, greater talent, more drive and ingenuity, and deep knowledge of the politics, culture, language, and economics of competitor nations became highly valuable—and prosperous. The finest athletes, writers, entertainers, technological innovators, financiers, motion picture directors, and corporate executives found themselves earning millions of dollars annually. They were often helped by marrying talented spouses, in a two-salaried arrangement that one observer has called "assortive meeting."[103]

The urgent need for increased talent, daring, and expertise profoundly transformed America's colleges and universities because the academic institutions were the primary producers of high-level skills for society. Universities went from the polite periphery to the vital economic and cultural center of society. More students sought to enroll in colleges, and more hoped to study business, or computer science, or a professional field rather than the liberal arts.[104] Working adults frequently chose to study in graduate programs or continuing education courses to upgrade their proficiency. Institutions broadened their curriculums.

The new American economy lifted the best professors

to new heights of affluence, influence, and importance. Entrepreneurs, the media, the military, and corporations all sought their views with increased frequency. Christopher Lasch noticed the change early, which he believed was "a social fact of prime importance: the rise of the intellectuals to the status of a privileged class." He noted that

> the post-industrial order created an unprecedented demand for experts, technicians, and managers. Both business and government, under the pressure of technological revolution, expanding population, and the indefinitely prolonged emergency of the cold war, became increasingly dependent on a vast apparatus of systematized data intelligible only to trained specialists; and the universities, accordingly, became themselves industries for the mass production of experts.[105]

Robert Frank and Philip Cook, in their 1995 bestseller, *The Winner-Take-All Society,* observed that "a superstar phenomenon—albeit a relatively mild one—has emerged in academia. Top researchers' salaries have escalated more rapidly than those of their lesser-ranked rivals, even as the teaching loads of top faculty have shrunk. The quest for academic prestige has also motivated universities to bid aggressively for top administrators, fund raisers, and others who have demonstrated the capacity to attract and manage resources."[106] For example, the presidents of the University of Michigan, University of Delaware, Vanderbilt University, and University of Texas system earn more than $700,000 annually in total compensation, and hundreds of other presidents and medical school deans receive between $500,000 and $700,000 each year.[107] The pay of dozens of corporate and financial executives now exceeds $100 million annually, which has recently brought a barrage of criticism from stockholders and the public.

In effect, much of the economy, and especially the finer colleges and universities, have become more meritocratic. The leading academic institutions now admit students mostly on the basis of high academic achievement and promise and downplay the importance of family, fame, and alumni connections. And since the wealthiest families often have children with the highest SAT scores and class standing, the nation's thirty-five to forty elite schools have increasingly become sanctuaries of the hardworking and most learned rich.[108]

The new socioeconomic class structure and America's new economy have helped reshape the country's higher education system into roughly four segments, each serving a distinct national need. The most prestigious is composed of the one hundred or so research universities, public and private, whose faculties are research-oriented; these universities are a copious source of new ideas, scientific findings, and discoveries, providing the country with cutting-edge knowledge to enable the U.S. economy to remain competitive in the face of low-wage competitor nations like China and Mexico. The most sentimentally revered segment is that of the small liberal arts colleges, which purport to train students for a broader, more historical, and aesthetic understanding, for leadership and public service, and for a global perspective. Teaching at the better of these 110 to 120 "academical villages" is often exemplary. The third segment is the huge, polyglot array of state colleges and universities, polytechnic institutions, proprietary schools, and regional, often underfinanced private colleges that prepare people to be accountants, nurses, schoolteachers, electronic experts, journalists, and the like. These institutions provide America with essential middle-range workers. Then there are the numerous two-year community colleges and struggling private colleges that serve several purposes: education for the underprepared, new immigrants, and adults, often for vocational tasks. These institutions enroll approximately 40 percent of all students in higher education.[109] Obviously, there are overlapping activities at many institutions in these four segments, but their direction and purpose are pointed.

At the other end of the new socioeconomic spectrum are the poor, whose household income has scarcely budged since the 1970s. The reasons given are frequently the competition from low-wage workers abroad, the tidal wave of immigrants, especially from Mexico, and the increase in single-parent or no-parent homes. But as the barriers for opportunity in America have been gradually torn away and as programs to aid the poor have multiplied, the causes of poverty have become more varied and are often said to be mostly self-inflicted: drug abuse, disdain for schooling and the failure to complete secondary school, alcoholism, criminal activities, lack of self-discipline, and reluctance to apply oneself to self-growth. A high proportion of the poor come from one-parent families, usually without a father, from among high school dropouts and drug addicts, as well as from newly arrived, uneducated immigrants.

Though the numbers vary, the evidence is clear that America has a rapidly growing number of multimillionaires, millionaires, and upper-income recipients, a middle-income group that is dwindling slightly, and a hard-core cohort of the poor, somewhere between 7 and

12 percent of the population, depending on who is counted. The new economy since the 1980s has put a premium on advanced education, traditional families, talent and higher-level skills, and certain kinds of personal behavior such as hard work, self-discipline, and entrepreneurship. And it has stymied those who lack these ingredients.

## Sociocultural Changes

The fourth major change in U.S. society since the 1970s has been the press toward full equality of opportunity for all. Alexis de Tocqueville long ago reported in his *Democracy in America:*

> Among the novel objects that attracted my attention during my stay in the United States, nothing struck me more forcibly than the general equality of condition among the people. I readily discovered the prodigious influence this primary fact exercises on the whole course of society. . . .
>
> I soon perceived that the influence of this fact extends far beyond the political character and laws of the country, and that it has no less effect on civil society than on the government; it creates opinions, gives birth to new sentiments, founds novel customs, and modifies whatever it does not produce.[110]

But America in the 1830s still had slaves. Women were seldom able to assume positions of importance or allowed into colleges. Some ethnic groups were derided. And the elderly were often left to die without medical help.

In the past few decades, however, the United States has taken many actions to open the doors of opportunity to all persons. The moves have been among the most significant ever in transforming U.S. society into a more fully egalitarian system. The most important change was the inclusion of and new support for black citizens, or African Americans. Beginning with the 1954 *Brown v. Board of Education* decision and continuing with the passage of the Civil Rights Act of 1964, the mandating of affirmative action, and the extraordinary leadership of Martin Luther King Jr., many of the nation's black persons have achieved close to integration. The median household income for blacks rose 27 percent in the 1990s, and black poverty declined 22 percent. College-educated black women did especially well. There are now several dozen African American mayors running major cities. The top executives at Merrill Lynch, Time Warner, American Express, and other large corporations have been blacks, as have been the last two U.S. secretaries of state. The numbers of black lawyers and college teachers have doubled since 1989; the numbers of black doctors, nurses, and managers have tripled. The number of African Americans enrolled in higher education has quintupled since 1970.

The situation is not all sunny. There are still pockets of racism and a need for constructive black leaders. The most disturbing element is the huge pool of young black males who are disconnecting from mainstream U.S. society. Fewer than 50 percent are completing secondary school, and nearly 70 percent of these dropouts are jobless, despite the growing economy. Approximately one-third of young black males are in prison, under indictment, or recent ex-offenders.[111] Two-thirds of all U.S. college students who are black are female.

The other major change has been the remarkable rise

of women in nearly all areas of American society since the early 1970s. In 1971, only 5 percent of the country's lawyers and judges and only 9 percent of doctors were women. There were few female architects, business leaders, dentists, or college and university presidents,[112] and there were almost no female engineers, physicists, U.S. senators, governors, economists, or philosophers. Since the 1970s the situation with women has altered dramatically, constituting one of the fundamental achievements of the "new" America. From 1970 to 2000 the number of women attending college rose by 136 percent, and they now make up 57 percent of all undergraduates. The increase at the graduate level is even larger; more than 300,000 more women than men enter graduate programs each year. Between 1970 and 2000, the percentage of women receiving medical degrees rose to 42.7 percent, the percentage of law degrees jumped to 45.9, and the percentage of M.B.A.'s leaped to 39.8. Two-thirds of all U.S. veterinarians and pharmacists are now female. The National Science Foundation reported that the number of females receiving Ph.D.'s in engineering rose from 1 percent in 1972 to 19 percent in 2002; in the physical sciences the increase was from 6 percent in 1972 to 29 percent in 2002. Half of all the Ph.D.'s in the life sciences and in humanities are now earned by women.[113] One commentator has observed that equal opportunity for women, especially in education, may be resulting in unequal results.

There are now more female U.S. senators and representatives than ever and more female governors of the states. Corporations such as eBay, PepsiCo, Archer-Daniels-Midland, Sara Lee, Xerox, Pearson PLC, and Lucent Technology are or have recently been headed by women executives, as are forty colleges and universities with the largest endowments, including three Ivy League universities. Egalitarianism has also been extended to handicapped persons, to gays and lesbians, and to immigrants, and Americans now spend more on the elderly and the poor than before.

The shift to near-total equality of opportunity has in turn brought several changes as consequences. For one, it appears to have increased the already high degree of individualism in the country. More young people have argued for "liberation" from all sorts of limits and restrictions—in family proscriptions, in manners, in religious allegiances, in speech and dress, and in rules and traditional mores in numerous areas. This change has given rise to what sociologist Daniel Bell has called "the antinomian self," where each individual is the source of his or her own moral behavior and judgment, based on an individual's view of personal and authentic identity, and is the creator of his or her own values, personality, appearance, and proclivities.[114] In the general culture there is a greater permissiveness, with violence, vulgarity, sacrilegion, and disrespect more prevalent. For higher education, this individualism erodes the idea of a common core of learning for all students and makes a college education that includes character guidance nearly impossible. And it has enhanced the proliferation of special instructional programs in black studies, women's studies, Chicano studies, gay studies, and others.[115]

But perhaps the most weighty—and terribly ironic—of the unintended consequences of the sociocultural revolution, which eliminated most barriers to advancement and greater life success for all, is the gradual formation of a new class structure for America. As the country has moved closer to becoming a meritocracy, those who take advantage of the new opportunities of greater egalitarianism through ambition, parental guidance, self-restraint, and hard work tend to get accepted to the better colleges and universities, obtain better-paying jobs, and receive more social respect and recognition. Those who fail to take full advantage of the radically new openness tend to earn much less and experience greater difficulties of many sorts. As attributes such as family background, race, religion, gender, occupation, and ethnicity decrease in importance, attributes such as cognitive ability, character, quality of performance, creativity, and social skills increase in value. Heredity emerges as a more significant factor.[116] Highly motivating persons and cognitive personal pilots and counselors, such as superb teachers, wise family members, religious leaders, close friends, and the authors of important books, also become more significant.

The greater stratification among citizens has ominous implications for those at the bottom of the new class structure. As Michael Young declared, "For the first time in human history the inferior man has no ready buttress for his self-regard."[117] The rich and successful become more arrogant and feel they are richly deserving, but the poor become more sulky, angry, violent, and self-destructive and wonder whom to blame. "Every year, it becomes more difficult to use any external barrier as an excuse."[118]

Thus, in the United States the advent of a new era of greater egalitarianism and meritocracy may be conducive to producing not just greater degrees of freedom and opportunity but also more pronounced socioeconomic differences among tomorrow's population.

# EDUCATION'S RESPONSE
# TO THE NEW SOCIETY

It is not the strongest species that survive, nor the most
intelligent, but the ones most responsive to change.

CHARLES DARWIN

I'm all for progress. It's change I don't like.

MARK TWAIN

IT NOW SEEMS CLEAR that American society has been
undergoing major changes in the past half century
and has experienced at least four huge transformations
since the 1970s, which may allow us to assert that there
is now a new America. Thus, the harsher critics of higher
education have a point. But have the nation's academic
institutions largely failed to notice the birth of the substantially different country that the United States has become? Have they too often been Luddites, disinclined to
adapt to the novel conditions of the new era, as numerous appraisers have alleged?

Some critics claim that most U.S. colleges and universities have been partially aware, at best, of the rapidly

changing conditions of their societal context and that only a very few institutions bother to monitor regularly the external environment in which they operate. Again, the critics of higher education have a point. Most academic persons focus mainly on their internal needs and difficulties, although many, especially those at the public colleges and universities, usually pay close attention to the outside political and financial sources of their support. Also, it is fairly widely agreed that colleges are neither nimble in their management nor eager to initiate changes. The governance of universities is usually unclear and frequently contested, as numerous studies have documented. As Ernest Boyer wrote in his 1987 inquiry, "Governance, on most campuses we visited, was an ineffective Rube Goldberg–like arrangement."[1] The muddled governance-management procedures and practices in U.S. higher education seriously hamper most institutions' ability to respond adroitly to novel conditions in society.

Yet, in some marvelous way, many of the nation's nearly four thousand colleges and universities have made alterations in response to each of the four transforming shifts since the 1970s, as well as to the changes in American religious practices and devotions, enlarging concerns for the physical environment and pollution, recent, less indulgent decisions toward academic autonomy by the courts, and the escalating costs of operation on their campuses. The allegation that U.S. higher education has done shamefully little to adjust to the different environment therefore seems hyperbolic. The charge, however, does contain a considerable sliver of substance. Why?

As we shall see, nearly all of U.S. higher education's

adjustments to the new environment have been incremental and within traditional structures developed a century ago. That is, the alterations have been beneficial in shoring up the viability of colleges and universities, but they have been cosmetic improvements, initiatives designed to help institutions respond to the major changes in society without having to begin a fundamental examination of their rusty old structures and delivery systems.

IN AN EXAMPLE of higher education's response to the radically new demographics of America, one can still see old admissions offices, often unattractive, located in basements, and without adequate signage to guide prospective students and their parents to the office. But most are now located prominently in the former homes of presidents, in one of a campus's loveliest houses, or in a new building where admissions, financial aid, and career counseling are jointly housed. Johns Hopkins University in Baltimore, to cite one illustration, has built a new four-level front door to its undergraduate campus, Mason Hall, which houses the visitor center. Historic photographs, faculty publication displays, and new, comfortable furniture now render many admissions offices inviting and informative. Some institutions' offices have videos on the academics, faculty, sports programs, and living arrangements at the school. The well-trained admissions staff members are usually genial and welcoming and now include black and Hispanic staff members, and many institutions use an expert on recruiting foreign students. Moreover, the admissions teams wander far more widely throughout their regions or even nationally; the University of Vermont now seeks applicants in the deep South, Midwest, and California. Some schools even have branch admissions offices in one or two distant locations. And there are strategic admission plans at numerous colleges to bolster the quality, diversity, and yield levels of each entering class.

In addition, institutions have been discounting their tuition prices and awarding "merit scholarships" based on exceptional academic promise or extraordinary talent in, say, athletics, music, or mathematics rather than strictly on financial need. Public universities, like the University of Florida, the University of Oklahoma, and Ohio State, and private universities and colleges, such as the University of Chicago, New York University, the University of Southern California, Carleton College, and Oberlin College, provide numerous National Merit Scholarships with their own money in addition to that of the National Scholarship Corporation. Nearly all institutions have improved their printed communications, sometimes based on careful market research, their Web sites, and their exchanges with the applicants. Other institutions have built alumni networks to help identify and woo prospects and have tripled the number of campus visits. Most colleges currently have retention programs and enrollment management procedures to assist with advising, roommate difficulties, extracurricular involvement, and the like. In summary, U.S. institutions have adjusted to the declining birth rates and to the fact that two-thirds of the growth in America's youth population in the coming decades will be Asian, black, Hispanic, Muslim, or American Indian.

Nor have a good number of the colleges and universities overlooked the growth in the number of elderly. By 2025 an estimated 20 percent of Americans will be older than sixty-five, triple the percentage of 1975. Already older persons make up one-third of all golfers in the United States and 60 percent of all cruise and travel vacationers. But the accredited U.S. colleges and universities, traditionally dedicated to educating younger persons (aged seventeen to twenty-five), have been slower to react to the explosive growth of adult and continuing higher education spurred by middle-aged and older citizens. Educating adults presents several obstacles. Most want to study part-time only, and many do not desire degrees or even credits for their courses. They often prefer to study in the evenings or on weekends. Their academic interests tend to be more work-oriented or highly specific. Instruction is expected to be less theoretical and with fewer lectures, and the instructors need to recognize the considerable experience that older students usually bring to class. Traditional faculty, accustomed to working with young people, are seldom successful as teachers of working or retired adults, and adjunct teachers who are practicing experts in their fields of work tend to be more popular.[2]

Nonetheless, beginning in the late 1970s, numerous colleges and universities scrambled to construct novel advanced-learning opportunities for working adults and retraining programs for those hoping to retool for the new and emerging economy. The two-year community colleges were the most responsive, but even the major universities soon cobbled new programs. Today, Harvard University and other noted institutions enroll more adults in continuing education than they do in all their harder-to-enter daytime schools. These adult education classes have become a new source of revenue for numerous institutions. New York University's School of

Continuing and Professional Studies brings in more than $92 million a year; Harvard earns about $150 million a year from adults, nearly 10 percent of the university's annual operating budget; the University of California in San Diego generates more than $25 million in revenue annually.[3]

The educational wants of older students are heterogeneous. Many merely want to add skills or credentials to help advance their careers, but others desire to enlarge their general knowledge, so the master of liberal studies degree, begun at Connecticut's Wesleyan University in 1953, has blossomed, from twelve programs in 1975 to more than two hundred today. A fair number of younger adults seek to earn their undergraduate degrees, and adult colleges such as DePaul's School for New Learning in Chicago, the University of Maryland's University College, Florida's Nova University, and the State University of New York's Empire State College have been created to serve them. Or universities such as New York University, UCLA, and Johns Hopkins in Baltimore have built huge, varied, and highly successful adult programs for their urban areas. Certificate programs of several months or a year in duration have been tailored for those who wish to learn some aspect of the newer crafts, say the operation of ultrasound machines or software program design. These programs' certifying exams measure the competence to perform in the workplace. The University of Washington in Seattle, for example, offers sixty-five certificate programs, both for credit and not for credit.[4]

In addition, there are Elderhostels, where older students can study a subject for a week or two at some accredited campus. Travel programs for adult groups to places such as historic Greece, the Inca ruins, or China and the Yangtze are now offered by several large universities, often led by a faculty member knowledgeable about the area and its cultural history. Dozens of leading business schools provide short, useful programs to executives and would-be executives in numerous cities in the nation and abroad, as well as on campus during weekends or in summer. Then, of course, many colleges and universities offer distance learning courses via computers to persons who learn at home. As many as one-fourth of all adults over thirty-five may now study annually, if part-time, in an adult program offered by some U.S. college or university.

Higher education has also made changes to accommodate the torrent of immigrants entering the United States since the early 1970s. In less than three decades the number of foreign-born persons in the United States has doubled from 6.2 percent in 1980 to 13 percent in 2005. Numerous colleges and universities have been attempting to include more of the new arrivals among their student populations, staff, faculty, and trustees and to create special programs for them. But higher education's efforts have been tentative and ill-fitting—for several reasons. For one, more of the immigrant young have not completed secondary school, and more are illegal entrants who usually do not qualify for scholarships or state tuition fees. For another, the willingness of immigrant groups to work hard to master American educational studies varies greatly.[5] Roughly one-fifth of the undergraduates at places like Princeton or Harvard are of Asian background, while the percentage of Latinos, blacks, and Filipinos is much smaller at these and most other institutions. There are language difficulties to be

overcome as well. Though Hispanics make up an estimated 52 percent of non–English speakers in the nation, the remaining 48 percent, or nearly half, speak
Chinese, Korean, Italian, Arabic, Hindi, Hebrew or Yid-
dish, or Vietnamese as their primary language. To increase the number of immigrant young, many colleges
have included them in their affirmative action initiatives, which has frequently angered African Americans.
As sociologist Orlando Patterson has complained about
this misuse of affirmative action: "It is absurd that all
South Americans and even persons from Spain, as well
as East Indians, Africans, and West Indians are among
the potential beneficiaries. America owes these people
nothing; giving them entry as immigrants is itself a privilege and gift. The [affirmative action] program should
be restricted to African Americans, Puerto Ricans, na-
tive Mexican-Americans, and Euro-American women."[6]

As for the dissolving nuclear family, here, too, some
U.S. colleges and universities have tried to find remedies for the growing number of financial, behavioral,
ethical, and aspirational difficulties brought to campus by
students from broken homes, fatherless families, and impoverished circumstances. Institutions have greatly increased their financial aid awards. Many have increased
their student affairs staffs to handle the volume of date
rapes, harassment, and plagiarism cases. Some schools
have introduced stringent speech codes to prevent ver-
bal attacks, though a few of the prohibitions have bor-
dered on the ridiculous. Most colleges have remedial or
developmental programs for freshmen with deficiencies. About 20 percent of entering students at public colleges and universities are required to take remedial
courses in, say, mathematics or reading to help overcome

deficiencies because of poor schooling or a lack of family guidance. Even most of the highly selective colleges have developmental courses annually for their talented but less disciplined new students. More positively, an increased number of institutions have expanded their communications with the parent or parents of their enrollees, something that many schools have neglected over the years since the early 1970s.

As for responding to the explosion of technological advances since the 1970s, U.S. colleges and universities have acted quite briskly. The response was often hesitant in the 1980s, but the introduction of the Internet and World Wide Web in the 1990s brought on huge investments in computers and their software by nearly all institutions. Today, most colleges have on-line registration, new cabinet officers called CIOs (chief information officers), links with other libraries, Web sites for admissions purposes, and e-mail systems for students and faculty. Research universities have sophisticated digital tools, as do medical, engineering, and architectural schools. Many campuses have set aside or built special buildings to instruct faculty and students in the latest use of the constantly changing new hardware and software. Smaller colleges have hired technical experts to assist with campus uses. The changes have been swift, expensive, and manifold.

But the digital outburst has given rise to new problems as well. For example, financial planning for information technology (IT) equipment, new personnel, and training has been ragged and in places insufficient. For professors who design a course for the Web or for distance learning, vexatious issues of who "owns" the course—professor, institution, or the public—have arisen. Intellectual property is a major new field.[7] Data on the Internet is not always reliable. Students can lift portions of digital presentations for inclusion in their analytical or interpretative papers for class and may be subject to charges of plagiarism. And there are the enormous costs for the new information technology, which often add to the pinched finances of most institutions.

Then there are the subtle losses of learning, as well as the numerous gains from the increased exchanges with other scholars and from the cornucopia of data available. No one has described these losses more sagaciously than John Seely Brown, the chief scientist of Xerox and co-founder in 1987 of the Institute for Research on Learning in Menlo Park, California. Here are some nuggets from Brown and his coauthor, Paul Duguid:[8]

> The knowledge-delivery view overlooks all the things that people learn on campus outside as well as inside the classroom. These can be as important to a student's career as teacher-delivered knowledge. People leave college knowing . . . not just academic facts, but knowing social strategies for dealing with the world. Reliable friendships and complex social strategies can't be delivered and aren't picked up through lectures, but they give an education much of its value.

> If, however, learning requires genuine participation, distance learning often provides its illusion only, while actually keeping students at a disempowering distance.

> Learning to be requires more than just information. It requires the ability to engage in the practice in question . . . Philosopher Gilbert Ryle . . . distinguishes

"know that" from "know how" . . . And "know how" does not come through accumulating information . . . "We learn *how*," Ryle argues, "by practice."

People don't become physicists by learning from formulas any more than they become football players by learning plays. In learning how to be a physicist or a football player—how to act as one, talk as one, be recognized as one—it's not the explicit statements, but the implicit practices that count . . . Learning involves inhabiting the streets of a community's culture.

We all need to learn things we didn't set out to learn.

The information economy, like the industrial economy, shows a marked indifference to people . . . The information economy threatens to treat them as more or less interchangeable consumers and processors of information. Attending to knowledge, by contrast, returns attention to people, what they know, how they come to know it, and how they differ.

The human and the digital are significantly, and usefully, distinct. Human planning, coordinating, decision-making, and negotiating seem quite different from automated information searches or following digital footsteps.

Perhaps the most fatuous and delusional expectation of information technology enthusiasts is that substituting IT for traditional teaching arrangements will enable colleges and universities to reduce their rising costs appreciably. Precisely the opposite has occurred. Indeed, wholly new higher education delivery systems have been created to replace existing instructional practices.

As a result, IT costs on most campuses have shot up from roughly 2 percent of instructional budgets in 1990 to more than 11–13 percent of the annual budgets today. Two leading scholars of higher education have found that "IT has actually driven up instructional costs . . . The upshot is that IT has emerged as a serious competitor for resources with and within academic affairs."[9]

Thus, U.S. colleges and universities have responded to the sudden and remarkable high-tech information explosion with considerable speed and expenditure, though not always with thoroughness or a clear sense of how best to employ the new forms of communication to further the learning of students. No one as yet seems to know how best to incorporate all the digital advances into higher education without losing essential and valuable elements of contemporary higher learning practices, which often work surprisingly well.

THE THIRD WEIGHTY SHIFT since the 1970s, the economy, has especially inflamed numerous business leaders, who are concerned most particularly about the sluggishness of American higher education to adjust, perhaps radically, to the emerging world economy and the new information society but also about higher education's own rising tuition prices and expenditures. A venomous example is the twenty-seven-page draft report of June 2006 from a national commission on higher education, appointed by U.S. Education Secretary Margaret Spellings and headed by Texas investor Charles Miller. This draft suggested that nearly every aspect of U.S. higher education needed to be renovated and rearranged. "Change is overdue," the nineteen-member commission and its staff concluded, alleging in an almost virulent tone that most American colleges and universities were derelict and reluctant to change.

The costs of attending classes in U.S. higher education have unquestionably increased since the late 1970s. According to the National Center for Education Statistics, tuition and fees for all four-your students in the United States rose from $3,167 in 1979–80 to $13,667 in 2001–2002. In real dollars, discounted for inflation, that rise was more than 250 percent. For major universities, the increase was nearly 300 percent, and for the nation's elite private universities and colleges, the charges rose even more. (The costs of enrolling at two-year colleges increased less than those at four-year schools.) Annual tuition increases since 2001–2002 have continued to exceed the yearly rise in inflation, so it now costs about forty thousand dollars a year to study at a leading private institution, more than one thousand dollars a week. And the costs at public universities are also rising as states can no longer afford to subsidize them as before.

Few issues in contemporary economics are less understood than the rising costs of higher education and similar fields. A disturbing flurry of legislative initiatives and recent articles and books by academics has failed to illuminate what is an underlying shift in highly developed, service-heavy economies. In a fundamental 1995 article, economists William Baumol and Sue Anne Batey Blackman wrote:

> The rapidly growing costs of higher education are not peculiar to the United States. Despite other industrialized countries' greater control over their university budgets, there are very few other advanced nations in

which similar complaints about the rates of cost increase for higher education are not heard. Indeed, the U.S. record is far from the worst. . . .

Moreover, the extraordinary rise in higher education costs is not unique. Much the same "cost disease" infects such other service fields as health care, legal services, library services, insurance, auto repairs, live artistic performances, police protection, fine restaurant meals, and a number of others.[10]

The rising costs in special service fields have been dubbed "Baumol's Disease" by savvy financial analysts because of his discovery and reminders of this development. The increased prices in higher education and similar important services are the effect chiefly of five components. One is the persistently slow growth in productivity in comparison with other activities in the economy. It is extremely hard to make a symphony orchestra or a library more productive. A second is that each of the rising-cost fields is labor intensive and demands personal attention. Consider medical treatments or gourmet restaurants, where standardization is resisted and labor cannot be reduced without a considerable loss of quality. No two automobile malfunctions are exactly alike. The third element is the requirement for highly expert personnel, who are usually expensive. When someone has a challenging legal case or a complicated problem of crime or terrorism, an experienced, knowledgeable, and skillful lawyer or police investigator seems a must. Fourth is the need in most of these fields for costly new equipment—for research scientists, oncologists and neurosurgeons, and theatrical performances. Fifth is the sheer and expanding demand for a scarce number of extraordinary people: superior chefs, librarians, economists, molecular biologists, historians, insurance actuaries, cellists, computer software designers. In sum, the costs of the newer highest-quality and creative services simply increase faster than do those of manufactured goods and services that do not call for much personal attention or a very high level of expertise. To quote Baumol and Blackman again: "Wasteful expenditures, greed, and poor management exist in higher education as they do elsewhere, but do not play the critical role."

America's colleges and universities have battled to contain the rising costs of operations, chiefly by seeking additional sources of revenue. They have raised tuition prices and the rents in their residential halls. Many have become more venturesome in investing their endowments, moving away from safe, conservative stocks and bonds toward alternative investments such as hedge funds, venture capital, real estate, international stocks, and commodities. For example, the College of Wooster in Ohio now has more than 70 percent of its endowment in hedge funds, and the University of Virginia devotes nearly 60 percent to hedge outfits. Stanford University has invested heavily in top-tier private venture-capital funds, striking gold with the soaring gains of Google, Inc., and advancing Stanford to third place in endowments, behind only Harvard and Yale, with $12.2 billion as of June 2005. Other schools have multiplied their endowments dramatically. From June 1992 to June 2005, Yale, with investing guru David Swensen at the helm, grew its endowment from $2.57 billion to $15.2 billion; Michigan State from $69.7 million to $906.3 million; Grinnell in Iowa from $292.9 million to $1.39

billion. Most colleges have also reduced the annual withdrawal from endowment for operations from 5 or 6 percent to 4 percent, and many institutions have had major drives to increase their capital funds. Pomona College in California has become a national leader in life income programs for the elderly and in donations from wills and estates.

To reduce expenditures many institutions have outsourced some noneducational enterprises—dining halls, bookstores, security forces, landscaping services, psychology and psychiatry offices, dormitories—to outside for-profit vendors. A growing group of academic institutions have been or are constructing conference centers, attractive inns, or small hotels to gain some new revenue, while a few others are building retirement villages near the campus for their older graduates or even setting aside burial plots for highly devoted former students. Numerous universities issue their own credit cards, from which they earn a portion of the profits. Others have cut deals with soft drink companies or sports equipment houses to sell their products exclusively in return for a slice of the sales receipts. Dozens of schools have offered early retirement plans to reduce their teaching and administrative staffs. Others, like Drexel University in Philadelphia, have begun using their technical and engineering expertise to create separate revenue-producing companies to help smaller colleges in the region with their computer and IT needs. Then there are the adult education programs and summer programs, which usually contribute surplus dollars. Research universities gain royalties from patents, developed by innovative faculty, an estimated $1.6 billion for all U.S. higher education in 2004. Universities such as

MIT, Columbia, California Institute of Technology, the University of Michigan, and Georgia Institute of Technology are perennial recipients of considerable dollars from patents, as are the multi-university systems of Texas, California, and Wisconsin. The United States spends more on university and corporate research than does any other country by far.

In reducing their costs, however, U.S. colleges and universities have been less effective. Decreases, curtailments, and phase-outs within an institution often produce protests and acrimony, which top administrators and leading faculty tend to steer clear of. Still, some resolute deans and academic vice presidents have closed down a few undersubscribed departments, such as those in linguistics, theater, Greek, Sanskrit, Latin, or Eastern European studies. Columbia ended its department of geography, Princeton its department of statistics, the University of Maryland its school of home economics. Numerous universities have cut their ambitious but severely underenrolled graduate programs in advanced mathematics, archaeology, hog science, and the like. And numerous colleges have reduced the proliferation of narrowly focused courses that some professors love to teach but that add little to student intellectual development—the philosophy of Martin Heidegger, a history of comic books, or women in the Ming dynasty. Several schools have eliminated a few of their sports teams, such as water polo, crew, or wrestling, although nearly all colleges and universities still spend 2 or 3 percent of their total budgets on intercollegiate athletics, which frequently suffers the greatest opprobrium of any aspect of their undergraduate operations.[11] And numerous coaches of Division I teams in football or basketball are paid from one to two million dollars a year.

But the principal way in which colleges and universities have tried to lower their expenditures has been through the swelling employment of part-time instructors in place of full-time faculty and the use, especially by the larger universities, of their graduate students as teachers of lower-class undergraduates. Part-time instructors seldom are provided separate offices, access to secretaries, telephones, computers, tenure, or full-time fringe benefits, which currently amount to 25 or 30 percent of salaries at most four-year institutions. Moreover, they are usually paid less than 50 percent of the amount paid to full-time professors.

The growth in the use of part-time instructors in U.S. higher education has been phenomenal. In 1980, non-full-time faculty may have been roughly one-fourth of the teaching force, located principally at two-year colleges. By 2004, at least one-half of all instruction at two- and four-year institutions was carried out by part-time faculty, graduate students, adjunct professors, visiting professors, and non-tenure-track hires.[12] Only one in four new faculty appointments in 2001 was to a tenure-track, full-time position. Tenure has not been abolished (except at a few schools), but it has been curtailed considerably as colleges and universities seek to reduce costs and gain greater flexibility in their staffing.

The part-time appointments are highly varied. They may be teachers of freshman composition or basic mathematics, of Mandarin Chinese or Russian, of graduate courses in finance or corporate accounting, or they may be hired to do research only at some specialized institute or to coach the golf or volleyball teams. They may be experts in school management, cardiology, or environmental science. They may teach horn-playing only for the music department or printmaking in the arts division. Many part-time persons have nearly full-time positions, and some are eminent experts outside of academe. A minority of part-time instructors have taught at their colleges for five or more years, especially if they are engaging and effective pedagogues. A majority of part-time instructors are appraised year after year by students as being highly student-oriented and helpful teachers.

THE FOURTH HUGE CHANGE, that of extending full opportunities to everyone in higher education regardless of race, gender, religious affiliation, ethnic origin, economic circumstance, or sexual preference (even advanced age or physical disabilities), began tentatively in the 1960s, following the Civil Rights Act of 1964, the Voting Rights Act of 1965, and the early stirrings of the women's movement. But progress was limited in the 1970s, although women advanced and the disabled benefited from a series of legislative acts facilitating their access to education and jobs. By contrast, in the 1990s and to this day, egalitarianism has become one of the most commanding drives in U.S. higher education, a nearly ubiquitous pressure on every segment of and activity in academe.

Academic buildings and entrances have been renovated to be handicap-accessible. New arrangements for aging professors were invented after 1994, when an amendment to the U.S. Age Discrimination in Employment Act ended the longtime practice of mandatory retirement for faculty at age sixty-five.[13] Numerous in-house studies have almost entirely corrected salary differences among faculty performing the same tasks. Hundreds of community colleges have been added since the 1970s to allow would-be students in every locale to attend a higher education institution near their homes, and public colleges have expanded and increased their repertoires. Students who are African American, Hispanic, or American Indian have at most institutions been recruited assiduously, and textbooks and histories of the United States have been rewritten to include the lesser known, unheralded, previously overlooked "little people" of America's past. Foreign students have been welcomed, as have the children of recent immigrants. New faculty, trustees, and staff are increasingly hired to give an appearance of full openness to equal treatment for all. Colleges have set aside more monies to assist students from modest-income families to pay for their college education, and numerous public institutions now waive their tuition fees entirely for the demonstrably poor. Gay and lesbian clubs are more frequently—though not yet pervasively—supported at U.S. campuses, as are Gay Pride celebrations.

More controversial and more academically significant is the egalitarian passion that has seeped its way into the content and instructional practices of courses and programs at many colleges and universities. As Alan Wolfe observed in 1994: "The emergence of political correctness in the late 1980s reveals a university bearing little resemblance to an earlier image of academic life. Far from cloistered, this university is politically engaged . . . The academy in the course of twenty years turned upside down."[14]

The increased politicalization of academe usually derives from a zeal to inculcate in students a particular view of social justice and egalitarianism and of the near-equality of the values of the world's many cultures. The devotion to leftish, partisan, often anti-American and anti–Western civilization, and pro-minority pedagogy, especially toward undergraduates, is certainly not universal in academe, but it is remarkably widespread and at some institutions pervasive. Steven Marcus, a former dean and academic vice president as well as a professor of English at Columbia University, noted recently: "America as a national society seems in the last generation or two to have arrived at something like a common decision: to use institutions of education—and in particular higher education—as a means for accelerating social change and mobility, redressing injustices, promoting various equalities, and enforcing cultural relativism."[15]

To cite only one example, Portland State University in Oregon offers a "capstone" course titled "Us and Them: A History of Intolerance in America." Hundreds of courses being taught today have a similar highly critical complexion based on what are alleged to be unremitting blockages by the nation to full equality, especially for a few minorities and the poor. Equally disturbing to some is the decline in treating each student as a thinking individual and the move to instead classify each of them as primarily a member of some group that merits improved justice and special treatments to produce total equality. Philosopher John Searle is an academic who is upset by this byproduct of egalitarian campaigns. To him, "the first assumption made by the challengers is that the subgroup into which you were born—your ethnic, racial, class, or gender background—matters enormously; it is important for education. In the extreme version of this assumption, you are essentially defined by your ethnic, racial, class, or gender background. This is the most important thing in your life . . . This is something new in American higher education."[16]

To Searle, one of the aims of a liberal education is "to liberate our students from the contingencies of their backgrounds" and invite them into membership in a much larger, more diverse, and worldwide intellectual or professional community. But for many passionate egalitarians, this traditional aim largely weakens the political bases for full equality battles on campus and creates a sense of false autonomy among individuals.

In effect, numerous professors have redefined the primary purpose of higher education. In their laudable desire to encourage their home institutions to become more socioeconomically equitable, to fall in line with American society's recent devotion to this goal, and to imbue their students with the commitment to full opportunities for every citizen, they have lifted political transformation above the age-old importance of objectivity, the pursuit of truth, and fairness to all sides of life's complex issues.

# WHAT'S NEXT
# FOR AMERICA'S COLLEGES
# AND UNIVERSITIES?

Imagination is more important than knowledge.

ALBERT EINSTEIN

The difficulty lies not in the new ideas but in escaping from the old ones.

JOHN MAYNARD KEYNES

M ANY, IF NOT MOST, of America's nearly four thousand colleges and universities have taken steps to react to the four formidable alterations in U.S. society since the 1970s. Contrary to some of the accusations, U.S. higher education has changed considerably in the past three decades. Institutions have improved their admissions and financial aid operations, installed new high-tech equipment and programs, broadened faculty and staff hiring and promotions, increased their services to adults and foreign students, modernized their curriculums (especially in the freshman year and in travel and study abroad), created strategic plans, and raised money aggressively to cope with the escalating costs of higher education.[1]

Numerous institutions have modified their practices in other areas of national concern as well. An example is academe's relatively new attention to improving the environment. Most campuses now recycle their paper and cardboard, which make up one-half of their waste, and more carefully dispose of their chemicals and other hazardous wastes. They have markedly reduced their energy usage, and thus their expenses on energy use, through better lighting, more controlled heating and cooling, and new furnace equipment. They have reduced the use of automobiles, and some have encouraged the use of bicycles. Nearly all colleges today have no-smoking areas, and a growing number buy local produce and purchase less-polluting paints, carpets, and other items. Campuses such as Tufts University, Brown University ("Brown Is Green"), and the Universities of Kansas, Missouri, and Wisconsin have ecological ombudsmen; Oberlin College has an Environmental Studies Center, as do several universities. And colleges and universities have more frequently employed "green" architecture in the construction of new buildings, at times including solar panels.[2]

Given all the adjustments and fresh initiatives of many of the traditional, accredited colleges and universities in the United States since the 1970s, what are we to make of the charges that these institutions have been reluctant and tardy to change in response to the new society or to the more fundamental suggestion that a radical restructuring of higher education is now imperative? A large number of institutions have made incremental changes and improvements in the past three decades. Many of the current initiatives of the colleges and universities are unknown, however, to the public and even to many in academe itself. The media scarcely cover higher education as a news area or report on its actions, despite the newly central role of advanced education and training in contemporary life. Few newspapers or news magazines have an education editor, and the coverage by radio and television is negligible. Much of what happens in U.S. higher education and among its fifteen million enrollees is unexplored territory for the media, except for collegiate sports, major personnel upheavals, and the occasional scandal.

But what about the more fundamental calls for major structural alterations for higher education? Are these mainly the recommendations of cranks, anti-intellectuals, and the mutinous? Or are they the profound observations of a small but discerning group of analysts (and some malcontents) who believe that the time has arrived for an overhaul of America's higher education enterprise? I think the latter has a strong claim to validity. In fact, it may be that only through considerable and profound restructuring can U.S. higher education continue to serve the nation in a powerful way. Here the more savvy critics of higher education have an insightful point.

Nearly all salutary changes that colleges and universities have made since the 1970s have been accomplished within the same structures as in the past. They are all merely incremental alterations within a century-old structure. And the existing structure is definitely an old one. Laurence Veysey, the finest historian of higher education in the late nineteenth and early twentieth centuries, wrote that "the decades between 1870 and 1910 witnessed the only genuine 'academic revolution' yet to be experienced in the United States. Most of the fundamental academic practices which continue to be familiar to us were first established in that period . . . The revolution of the late nineteenth century quite simply created the American university (and the undergraduate college) much as we now know them."[3]

Before the late nineteenth century, U.S. colleges had no academic departments or majors, no deans or strong presidents, few professional schools, scanty electives, almost no research or graduate programs, virtually no academic attention to the world of work, no numbered courses or a credit system, no tenure, no alumni associations or organized fund raising. Most classes were run mainly as recitations by the students, and there were almost no informed lectures by the professors and no seminars. Colleges were small, with only a few hundred students or fewer, and enrollments were not increasing. But in the forty years or so around the turn of the twentieth century, a radically new structure was put in place, one that still remains and is now largely unquestioned and widely regarded as obviously proper and orthodox.

The academic transformation of 1870–1910 was propelled by several factors. One was the desire by many farmers, industrialists, workers, and people of commerce to scrap the heavy emphasis on Latin, Greek, and Christian pedagogy and replace it with a more utilitarian view, connecting higher education more closely with the actual conditions of the emerging American economy. The passage of the Morrill Act of 1863, establishing land-grant colleges, which required instruction in modern agricultural practices, "mechanical arts" or engineering, and military service, kicked off extensive educational reforms at the state universities especially but altered instruction at many private institutions as well.⁴ Another factor was the more elitist new emphasis on archival, empirical, and experimental research, influenced considerably by the German universities and the increasingly intellectual interests of a more scientifically oriented minority of faculty. This factor led quickly to the growth of graduate schools after Yale established the first American Ph.D. degree in 1863. In 1876, a new kind of university was started in Baltimore, Maryland, through the seven million dollar beneficence of railroad baron Johns Hopkins, emphasizing research almost exclusively.

A third element was the rise of a management structure in the colleges and universities, prodded by the formation of new schools of business, agriculture, law, medicine, pharmacy, dentistry, nursing, engineering, even forestry and mining; by the increased enrollments in the late 1800s, which enlarged the universities (by 1910, Chicago, Columbia, Cornell, Illinois, Michigan, and Penn State each had more than four thousand students); and by the sudden need to design and build a new kind of university and to raise money for growth and research facilities. Deans of the professional schools appeared, as did powerful and innovative presidents, such as the University of Chicago's William Rainey Harper, Columbia's Nicholas Murray Butler, Cornell's Andrew Dickson White, Harvard's Charles Eliot, Johns Hopkins's Daniel Coit Gilman, and Stanford's David Starr Jordan.

A fourth factor was in part an annoyed reaction to the growing emphasis on the sciences, research, and graduate and professional schools and in part a strategy to keep many of the ideals of the old-time college alive but without the onerous stress on the classics, the inculcation of religious virtue, and the use of unscholarly faculty. Called the liberal arts or general education, the programs became the bedrock of America's smaller colleges and a few universities such as Princeton, which chose not to add professional schools. A fifth factor was the surprising outpouring of monies to the colleges and universities from the newly rich of modern industrialism. Philanthropists suddenly donated millions to start colleges for women, for new professional schools, and to construct campus buildings.[5] And the more ambitious presidents became more aggressive about soliciting funds from the affluent. "Captains of erudition" was the moniker some gave them.

State legislative leaders likewise began to support their embryonic state universities. Between 1875 and 1910, city, state, and federal revenues to higher education rose from $667,521 to $24,528,197, while gifts to campuses by individuals jumped from $2,703,650 to $18,737,145, according to the annual reports of the U.S. Commission of Education.[6]

As U.S. colleges and universities sought to transform themselves to respond to the new industrial economy, the different culture, and the growth of the sciences and international connections, they did a remarkable thing. They adopted all five of the components pressing for change. Universities became more vocational and restructured themselves to prepare more students for the world of work and the professions. Faculties conducted more research, institutions enlarged their instruction in the sciences, and scholars dug into original documents and historical actions with fresh fervor. Many colleges revised their liberal arts requirements and forms of pedagogy. Nearly all the institutions modernized their management organizations, adding subordinates and associates. And numerous colleges and universities altered their boards of trustees to include more successful entrepreneurs, and they instituted several other fund-raising practices to gather new monies.

Thus, much of American higher education transformed itself with three new educational aims, led by a stronger central management, and with an unabashed new pluralism of academic emphases. The trio of educational purposes—to prepare the young for occupations and professions useful and important for the nation; to infuse students with a sense of service and the significance of character and to familiarize them with the finest achievements of humankind and their own national heritage; and to encourage and assist them in methods of creating new knowledge—actually reflects an age-old tension. More than twenty-three hundred years ago, Aristotle, in searching for the best ingredients for training youth, found that

> at present opinion is divided about the subjects of education. All do not take the same view about what should be learned by the young . . . If we look at actual practice, the result is sadly confusing. It throws no light on the problem whether the proper studies to be followed are those which are useful in life, or those which make for goodness, or those which advance the bounds of knowledge. Each sort of study receives some votes in its favor.[7]

The three aims—preparation for work, for well-rounded and deeply grounded learning, and for research and scholarship—are still those of many U.S. academic institutions, alongside such more recent aims as greater attention to the environment, social justice, international understanding, and an enlarged sensitivity to religious, multicultural, racial, and gender differences. The multiplicity of educational goals has complicated the choices, confused many students, and made life much more perplexing for regular faculty, yet each of several educational purposes of contemporary higher education seems necessary and valuable.

Just as important, the structure of U.S. institutions of higher education is much the same as it was in 1915, more than ninety years ago. A college education is still four years in length, with a proliferation of courses for credit available and approximately 120 credits required for graduation. Academic inquiry is still broken up into separate departments, each of which has essentials for something called a major. There are still usually two semesters a year, from early September to late May, a holdover from America's agricultural past. There are still faculty who are expected to teach, conduct research or engage in scholarship, advise students, perform campus or public service, and often win tenure. Graduate programs are still devoted mainly to preparing research-oriented scholars, with no formal introduction into the craft of teaching in the classroom. Universities have approximately the same professional schools as in 1915, with deans managing them. Many institutions still have liberal arts requirements, especially for breadth, though liberal arts programs have often become frayed, controversial, and avoided by senior professors.[8] And U.S. institutions still are heavily influenced by presidents and a cadre of vice presidents. In effect, U.S. colleges and universities have made numerous incremental and positive changes in response to the radically new situation they now face, but they have done so almost entirely within a nearly century-old structure of the delivery of higher education, to which they cling with extraordinary tenacity.

THAT THE UNITED STATES has entered a markedly different society with novel characteristics and challenges suggests that higher education's incremental changes, however imaginative and adventurous, are no longer sufficient. The changes and new developments are so prodigious and fundamental that only a major renovation of the turn-of-the-century academic structures can allow U.S. colleges and universities to maintain their animating and central role in the emerging new America. This basic shift—from incremental improvements, whether larger fund drives, new strategic directions, or different faculty hiring practices, to the need for a bold, inventive structural overhaul of higher education—may be what some of the more acerbic critics are calling for. Certainly a small collection of the more perspicacious of higher education observers contends that an overhaul is necessary.

The most farsighted scholar of higher education's new predicament, Martin Trow of the University of California at Berkeley, long ago perceived that America's increased emphasis on wider access to higher education, with more than half of all secondary school graduates going to college instead of the traditional 15 or so percent, would require internal changes in academe and probably a major redesign of the structures and variety of higher education. In a penetrating book chapter written more than thirty-five years ago, Trow predicted that America's moves to mass higher education "will lead within the next decade to very large changes in the character of higher education in this country" and warned that "the future of higher education cannot be an extrapolation of past tendencies."[9] In 1994, two university presidents, Harold Shapiro of Princeton and his brother Bernard Shapiro of McGill University in Canada, wrote an unpublished paper in which they said, "The challenges at present relate to neither whether nor how to develop a mass higher education system but rather how to structure these systems for a new age."[10] Other observers, such as former university presidents James Duderstadt of Michigan and Richard Freeland of Northeastern, and a few scholars of higher education, such as K. Patricia Cross, Alexander Astin, and Clara Lovett, have also recommended considerable structural alterations, as have knowledgeable outside analysts such as John Seely Brown and Michael Gibbons, secretary general of the Association of Commonwealth Universities.[11]

Recently two of America's top scholars of faculty conditions have declared, "American higher education and the academic profession that serves it are on the edge of an unprecedented restructuring that is changing the face—indeed, even the very meaning—of higher learning."[12] Two leading analysts of business strategies have argued that "we've reached the limits of incrementalism." To them, today's strategic planning "is essentially incremental tactical planning"; instead, the task now is "to imagine a future made possible by changes in technology, life style, work style, regulation, global geopolitics, and the like."[13] In my interview with former Northeastern University president Richard Freeland, he said, "We have not changed our structure, pedagogy, staffing, and academic contents adequately to match all the new developments. We need greater social invention in U.S. higher education."

From several quarters, then, two facts have become more widely recognized: that since the 1970s the United States has entered a new age and that the nation's colleges and universities urgently need to break out of their century-old structures and redesign the delivery of advanced education and training for the new age. Those who advocate major renovations to the existing structure of higher education are still a relatively small group, but the pressures to undertake such renovations are mounting. The tendency to prefer incremental improvements within the current structure increasingly smacks some critics as eerily similar to the long-held belief in the epicycles of the Ptolemaic system before the acceptance of the heliocentric Copernican system in the sixteenth century.

What are the emerging pressures on higher education that seem to demand a fundamental reconstruction of the old and familiar structure? They are abundant.

The most significant is what has been infelicitously dubbed "massification," or the movement from college and professional training for a relatively small and fairly well-motivated percentage of the nation's young to a greatly enlarged range of higher education services for approximately 60 percent of all U.S. secondary school graduates. This is the expansion of access that, as Martin Trow foresaw in the 1970s, would require a wider variety of institutions and different kinds of pedagogy, faculty, and academic objectives. The traditional American college or university, devoted largely to a combination of the British model of teaching a residential population and the German model of von Humboldt's emphasis on research for a small elite, is no longer suitable for the less academically prepared or less motivated mass of new degree-seekers. The United States is not alone in the massification of higher education. The number of persons attending universities has swelled throughout Europe, Mexico, and other countries. India doubled its attendance between 1990 and 2005, and China is engaged in the largest university expansion in history.[14] The desire of growing numbers of young people to participate in higher education raises a multitude of new issues and basic structural, financial, and academic difficulties.[15]

Almost as significant is the so-called IT revolution, or the transfiguring consequences of the computer and its software, especially the Internet. The radically new technologies demolish the near-monopoly once held by colleges and universities of vital information, data, and international connections; shatter the need for much on-site learning, except for collaborative research and professional training; permit asynchronous education and greater exchanges among universities and their professors and between students and their teachers; and much more. The introduction of the new information technology demands a comprehensive renovation of traditional on-campus classroom lectures, modes of academic inquiry, research techniques, and instruction.

Also complicating the customary work of colleges and universities is a throng of new competitors who teach, conduct research, and publish new findings. Assisted considerably by the new modes of digital investigation and data delivery and by the mounting avidity among many for the latest new developments and information, numerous "think tanks," as they are often labeled, have sprouted to collect and print out data, suggest trends, and even recommend policies and courses of action based on their findings. Most are not connected to universities and are independently financed, often competing with university scholars for research grants and major gifts. But the profusion of new competitors has come largely in the area of teaching.

Among the worst-taught subjects in academe have been foreign languages. Now there are outside firms like Rosetta Stone and several others competing to help develop fluency, fairly quickly, in spoken Arabic, Chinese, French, Hindi, and a dozen or more languages. Brigham Young University has long had an eight-week crash course in fifty or so languages, cultures, and religions for its Mormon students, who are expected to do missionary work. And numerous colleges and universities have built or set aside on campus language houses, where only a foreign language is spoken. In effect, intensive practice, immersion, and emphasis on spoken language rather than on literature have sprung up to compete with the older and fruitless modes of instruction.

Nearly two thousand corporations, from Harley-Davidson to Microsoft, offer courses, as do a growing number of companies in other countries. Museums now deliver courses in the arts, and higher education organizations, from the American Council on Education to the Society for College and University Planning, present courses for their members annually. And roughly eighty for-profit companies deliver basic data and information to approximately 1.6 million students, mostly working adults but baccalaureate seekers, too. Their enrollments are growing faster than enrollments at traditional universities and may now compose as much as 8 or 9 percent of all U.S. college and university students by head count. As Michael Gibbons has noted, "A multi-billion dollar industry has developed outside established education institutions, responding in more direct, and usually more effective ways to the needs of industry and the labor market."[16]

One of the more inventive and attractive of the new competitors in teaching is a Virginia-based firm called the Teaching Company. The principals comb the nation's superior colleges and universities to identify the finest teachers in fields such as statistics, ancient Greek civilization, astronomy, the New Testament, calculus, elements of jazz, economics, and classical music and sell their lectures and illustrations in audio and video form. Buyers can thus build their own liberal arts package of courses taught by America's most outstanding professors. The new competitors to higher education seem multitudinous. Wyoming's Yellowstone National Park, for example, has a Yellowstone Institute, which presents field courses each summer on wildflowers, geology, Indian history, and fly-fishing. The Fifth Avenue Presbyterian Church in New York City has opened a Center for Christian Studies, with instruction in such areas as church history, practical theology, and drama. Teaching has been a remarkably fecund activity throughout the country, reducing the role of colleges and universities and squeezing them into a limited, more specialized function in society.

The clientele of higher education has been transformed. Not only are there more women, minorities, foreign students, and immigrant young enrolled in most colleges and universities, but the basic constituency of traditional higher education—young men and women aged seventeen to twenty-four—is being expanded and gradually matched by a relatively new constituency: adults aged twenty-five to seventy. Adults currently have swelled to nearly 40 percent of all enrollees and could increase to one-half in the coming decades. U.S. higher education now is compelled to serve two clienteles, not one as in the past. And the two have very different needs. Many colleges and universities have attempted to cope with the flood of adult students since the 1970s but mainly in a spotty add-on to their traditional youth programs. One expert in adult education, Kay Kohl, has written that

> the current higher education system is not structured to accommodate the needs of a lifelong learning society. Universities are important providers of executive education and vocational master's degree programs— often lucrative endeavors. Yet it is postbaccalaureate certificate programs that evidence job-related competence and on-line courses tailored to changing workforce needs that are increasingly in demand. . . .
>
> In a very real sense, the postbaccalaureate learning imperative is compelling traditional universities to reexamine their entire system in the context of the emerging knowledge economy. What function does the university serve? Whom does it educate?[17]

Perhaps the most profound pressure for structural change—and the most upsetting to many faculty members—is the gradually changing connection between business, corporate research, the personnel needs of the emerging economy, and the traditional values of academe. Indeed, many articles and books have recently deplored how the life of profits and the life of the mind are drawing closer together every year. In the emerging knowledge economy, business firms must have more knowledgeable workers, smarter executives, and better products and research, and an enlarging majority of college students want an education that prepares them for work in tomorrow's economy. But some professors prefer to deconstruct the writings of, say, Shakespeare or Jane Austen or recount the oppression and neglect of women in past centuries, while others want undergraduates to know their Western heritage in the arts, philosophy, politics, religion, science, and great literature.

A major upheaval in the traditional devotion of universities and their faculties to the transmission of knowledge and faculty-driven curriculums and courses is taking place, however. The very purpose of most of U.S. higher education is being transposed. Michael Gibbons describes the transposition with directness:

> During the past twenty years, a new paradigm of the function of higher education in society has gradually emerged. Gone, it seems, is the high-mindedness of a von Humboldt or a Newman, with its pursuit of knowledge for its own sake. In their places has been put a view of higher education in which universities are meant to serve society, primarily by supporting the economy and promoting the quality of life of its citizens. While it is true that universities still retain their role as the "conscience of society," the critical function of universities has been displaced in favour of a more pragmatic role in terms of the provision of qualified manpower and the production of knowledge . . . The new paradigm is bringing in its train a new culture of accountability . . . In all countries, developed or developing, the culture of accountability is going to become more and more firmly established . . . [and] relevance will be judged primarily in terms of outputs.[18]

The traffic between economic interests and higher education has been swelling. Numerous institutions have contracted to train or upgrade the workers at nearby companies. Universities have built industrial parks close to their campus for start-up businesses and corporate research. Entrepreneurship is now taught at many business schools. And more professors each year do consulting, part-time work, or research for corporations, especially in fields such as the life sciences,[19] or leave their university positions to start their own business. Indeed, it was American institutions that pioneered in forging links between the academic world and industry.

Some of the links, however, are becoming invidious. For example, in 1998 the Novartis drug and biotech company signed a $25 million contract with the University of California at Berkeley to conduct research guided by an oversight committee with two members of Novartis and three from UC-Berkeley, and Novartis can license the discoveries and delay publication of the research findings. Clemson University in South Carolina opened an International Center for Automotive Research in 2006, becoming the first U.S. university to award a doctorate in automotive engineering. The center was made possible by a $10 million gift by the German automaker BMW to Clemson, which allows BMW to help develop the course of study, suggest professors and practicing engineers, and even approve the new school's architectural look.[20] Michelin and the Timken Company, a bearings manufacturer, have also contributed, and the state has donated $25 million to build the graduate school. Companies such as Sun Microsystems and Google, among others, were developed by Stanford scholars and graduate students, as were companies in the Boston and Austin, Texas, areas.

ANOTHER MAJOR DEVELOPMENT that must be faced is the steady increase in the charges for attending private and public colleges and universities. Several polls have revealed that many Americans now regard the rising costs of higher education to be as worrisome as the escalation in health care costs, the persistence of crime, or the threat of terrorist attacks. Tuition charges since the early 1980s have risen faster than the increases in median family income, and they continue to rise more than the Consumer Price Index annually. Total expenses at the best private research universities and liberal arts colleges in America approached forty-five thousand dollars in 2007, and most of the better public university costs are two-thirds of that sum.

More and more state legislatures, national commissions, and members of the public are urging institutions to lower the annual increases in tuition and increase financial assistance. But colleges and universities have great difficulty in reducing their tuition revenue. The salaries of the most promising and productive professors keep rising, as do the expenses for IT, new sports facilities, improved science buildings and equipment, and entries into other fields such as the arts and communications (television, film, etc.). So further financial tinkering within the century-old structure of higher education is no longer sufficient, and structural renovations seem imperative.

Also, colleges and universities that offer graduate programs probably need to recast them for the new age. A good number of master's degree programs have already been redesigned to provide competence in non–liberal arts fields, which Steven Brint calls "the practical arts," a shift, he says, that "represents an important change in American higher education."[21] But most Ph.D. programs, especially at leading research universities, are still aimed exclusively at preparing students for research activities. Teaching undergraduates is definitely not part of the doctoral training, though a good percentage of Ph.D. candidates do get asked to help teach freshmen and sophomores while they are working on their dissertations. What this means is that most doctoral programs are still fixated on turning out a new generation of research scholars with little or no attention to teaching.

Ronald Ehrenberg, professor of economics and director of the Higher Education Research Institute at Cornell University, who served three years as the university's vice president for programs, planning, and budgeting, remembers that

> many Cornell faculty [especially in the College of Arts and Sciences] believe that the primary purpose of the university is to conduct research and educate undergraduates and Ph.D. students on campus. They saw calls by the administration to get them involved in professional master's programs and distance learning as indicative that the administration had different values than they did. Some viewed such calls as evidence of a battle for the very "soul" of the university.[22]

But of America's more than thirty-eight hundred accredited colleges and universities, only fifty or sixty would be considered premier research universities like Cornell. At the 3,740 other colleges and universities, teaching, not research, is most important. This is particularly so because of the "massification" of higher learning, where most of the entrants to state colleges, comprehensive universities, and community colleges are unlikely to be interested in original research and its techniques but are desirous of becoming more educated generally and learning how to make a living in some field. Thus, for the overwhelming majority of today's higher education students, superior, eye-opening, and rousing instruction, in the classroom and on-line, is the urgent and fundamental requirement for most of the faculty.

Yet most graduate programs pay almost no attention to teaching and its better elements. Worse, many schools of education, both undergraduate and graduate, devote little zeal to training in the ingredients for superior lecturing, seminar interrogations, or directed discussion. Thus, greatly increased access has hugely expanded the need for teaching in higher education, yet colleges and universities have preferred to cling to the older, more traditional practices of a pre–mass higher education era, and many ordinary colleges and universities still call for a research-driven Ph.D. from their new and tenure-track hires as teaching faculty.

YET ANOTHER SHIFT that affects all U.S. colleges and universities is the rise of new power centers in the world. Traditionally, U.S. academic programs have concentrated on Western civilization from the Greeks, Romans, and Europeans to the present. They have taught, sometimes extremely well, about the past and the origins of logic, art, mathematics, music, religion, science, and great literature in Western cultures, as well as about the rise of systems of democracy, the rule of law, egalitarianism, and capitalism, which are all products of Western peoples.

But since the 1970s new centers of economic production, culture, and power have risen in East Asia from South Korea, Japan, and China to Singapore, Taiwan, and India. The Near East, especially Israel, Palestine, and the surrounding nations, has become an increasingly violent battleground, and three-fifths of the world's known oil supply is located under the surface of Near Eastern countries. Humanitarian concerns have expanded for Africa, a potentially rich continent afflicted by disease, racial and tribal hatreds, kleptocratic governments, murderous rulers, and widespread poverty.[23] In addition, an apparent worldwide war has broken out among a minority of radical and violent Muslims who despise Western and particularly American moral laxity, prosperity, military might, pluralism, and Christian and Jewish religions.[24] Roughly one-fifth of the world's population is devoted to the Islamic faith, yet most Americans are taught little about the teachings of the Koran or the several strands of Muslim religious piety.

How does a college teach undergraduates about the various new world conditions while maintaining a focus on the key elements of Western history, achievements, and civilization; on American values, scientific emphases, pluralism, and individualism; and on the burgeoning demand for excellent training in numerous fields of work? Where does U.S. higher education acquire faculty broadly concerned with larger, emerging issues when young scholars are pressed to specialize and become research-oriented searchers in some one, well-defined area of knowledge? What is a "liberal education" in the new era?

What is next for America's colleges and universities in the face of these shifts and transformations since the 1970s? Surely they must redesign their structures in some fundamental ways to respond to the new challenges to their primacy, traditional practices, academic emphases, and conventional attitudes. Incremental improvements are clearly insufficient for the radically new era that the United States has entered.

# REMODELING
# THE KINGPIN

He that will not apply new remedies must expect new
evils; for time is the greater innovator.

FRANCIS BACON

We have met the enemy, and he is us.

WALT KELLY

NOTHING IS HARDER, as Niccolò Machiavelli and
numerous other keen observers have pointed out,
than initiating a new order of things. Restructuring is always extremely difficult. In the field of higher learning,
it seems nearly impossible. Yet it was done in higher
education a century ago, and today's radically new conditions, societal transformations, different students, and
changing academic interests in the United States seem
to demand a replay of the fundamental 1870 to 1910
overhaul at America's colleges and universities. Actually, in a few areas of activity, the higher education enterprise has already begun drifting into new patterns of service and content. The restructuring is actually under way.

What are some of the areas in U.S. higher education structures that must be considered and perhaps changed? With considerable uneasiness, I offer several, in no order of priority, but each is based on the transformations in society I have described. The formidable changes since the 1970s are remarkably similar to the scope and weight of the shifts in society of the 1870–1910 period in America, so these suggestions for structural alterations seem timely.

## Adjust to Segmentation

Probably the most compelling structural change is that of redesigning U.S. higher education to respond to the country's dogged emphasis on access for everyone possible to enroll in some form of collegiate and continuing education. This view is promoted widely and sometimes vociferously because the new information-rich, global economy is said to require a more educated populace and because the intensified adherence to egalitarian outcomes means that no one should be excluded from higher learning in some form. Elitism is generally considered a contemptible and cruel yearning, an absence of fairness.[1] The necessity is therefore to structure America's higher education system for a mass of students who range from the brightest, most gifted, and intellectually keen to those who mainly want a good job and are underprepared for demanding undergraduate studies.

The standard notion of a college or university as a residential home for selected, bright students of promise taught largely by scholarly and research-oriented faculty in the liberal arts and within the niceties of a disciplinary field pertains today to only a tiny minority—

perhaps 5 or 6 percent—of enrollees in U.S. higher education. Astonishingly, however, this outmoded idea of "college" persists. Many persons in society, from journalists and political leaders to parents and leading professors, still carry in their heads an erroneous idea of what is prevalent in higher education. Whether from the *New York Times* or the *San Francisco Chronicle* or the pundits who write about U.S. higher education, this is the elitist view of higher education the egalitarian commentators describe and fret about. Who writes, or worries about, the North Dakota State College of Science, Daytona Beach Community College, Alabama's Troy University, Stonehill College in Massachusetts, or Concordia University in Oregon? Yet institutions such as these today make up more than 90 percent of U.S. higher education. Massification prevails, and the current structure should reflect this development.

Surprisingly, American higher education has to some extent restructured itself to accommodate the much wider range of student abilities and interests. Most evident is the gradual drift since the 1970s of the nation's traditional colleges and universities into four relatively distinct sectors of academic service to meet the greater breadth of student preferences and styles and to fulfill national demand. The breakup was not part of some grand long-range federal or One Dupont Circle plan, although specific federal and state economic incentives were extended for, say, academic research and for financial assistance for the poor. But a new segmentation has indeed occurred, and a clear understanding of this segmentation is essential for any further analysis or action.

The four sectors are, first, the sixty to eighty major research universities that U.S. journalists, ambitious parents, and most higher education scholars love to emphasize. These universities provide America with many of its new findings and concepts. They help keep the United States in the forefront in medicine, history, technology, economics, philosophy, ecology, and much more. Several are hailed as the finest universities on earth. They harbor a majority of the country's most brilliant academic researchers and intellectuals and many of the brightest undergraduate and graduate students, and they possess superb libraries, electronic gear, and science facilities. Though they compose only 2 percent of America's colleges and universities, their influence on society is immense. But the intense concentration on research usually results in a painful neglect of undergraduate teaching, liberal learning, and student counseling.

The second sector is also small and it is contracting: the liberal arts colleges. Their number has dropped from 721 in 1970 to 400 or so in 2004, according to the Carnegie categories, but the actual number may be no more than about 110, and enrollments in these colleges have decreased nearly 10 percent. The liberal arts colleges carry on the tradition of educating young people in the great achievements of the past—its philosophies, military adventures, religious beliefs, arts and literature, scientific advances, and political theories and forms. The goal of liberal arts colleges is to educate broadly persons of critical, appreciative, and historically grounded intellect, to produce graduates with wide perspectives, high standards, and a creative bent. Leadership and public service are often supplementary advocacies.[2] As W. Bruce Leslie says, the American liberal arts college is "unique. No European educational system has a similar institution."[3] But the pressures among the young to prepare for work, a career, or a profession or to obtain specific training are mounting. So to some, a liberal arts college education seems an aristocratic indulgence or, at best, an advantageous grooming for graduate school; to others, it is seen as perhaps a useful baccalaureate education for the new global, multicultural, rapidly changing world.

The faculty at this thin layer of colleges are widely knowledgeable and tend to be collegial and active in campus policy decisions but are becoming scarcer. A dozen or so colleges contain serious scholars and researchers, but most mainly have good or superb teachers who have scholarly standards but only a modicum of new knowledge productivity or a flair for graceful prose. Students at this tier of institutions are often made aware of the achievements of the Greeks, the Arab contributions in the ninth to twelfth centuries, and the Renaissance painters, as well as the growth of modern science and the major economic, political, and religious developments in the West since Chaucer, Thomas Aquinas, and Elizabeth I. There is much talk of "the life of the mind," accompanied by a frequent disdain for commerce and vocationalism. As president of Oberlin College, E. H. Wilkins said, back in 1927, "Every potential leader, then, and no one else, should go to college."[4] Some of today's professors at liberal arts colleges would almost agree, contending that instruction in hotel management, dental technology, or bookkeeping is hardly the work of the American college. The liberal arts colleges thus educate a slice of the young in the larger realm of ideas, great art, history, and the basics of experimental science, a not-so insignificant contribution in a time of spreading vocationalism and lack of historical outlook.

The third kind of institution is huge in both number and size, with tens of thousands of undergraduate and graduate students occasionally assembling at a single university such as Ohio State University or the University of Florida. These institutions—state colleges and universities, regional private colleges and universities, colleges of technology, and the newer for-profit universities—are principally devoted to training young persons for the world of work in a wide variety of fields from nursing, business, and agriculture to engineering, teaching, and applied art. The sector is a vital mainstay for providing skilled workers and officers for the diverse needs of America's capitalist economy. There often remain some liberal arts requirements at many of these career-oriented universities.

Fourth is the sector composed of the seventeen hundred two-year colleges, proprietary (privately or corporately owned) schools, and many of the least well-endowed colleges, which often accept underprepared applicants who tend to be heavily job oriented. The work of the faculty in this sector is in many cases upsetting and difficult, since the students often have difficulties and tend to be languorous; vocational instruction is challenging for many traditional instructors; and traditional teaching methods (lectures, seminars, and discussion groups) are often not appropriate.[5] But a surprising amount of academic rescue work and lighting of fires takes place in this sector, which primarily serves the nation with occupational expertise, better grammar, and help and guidance for the less able and often neglected poor and newer immigrant young.

Thus far no other country has begun to restructure itself for the massification of higher education as has the

United States so that it can educate students from the most undereducated and practical to the most brilliant and conceptual. In this arena, America has pioneered with its four sectors. Several other nations, however, have begun to open more two-year colleges, private universities, and colleges of technology, art, and education to handle the widening range of student abilities.

The four-tier arrangement in American higher education nevertheless remains rudimentary and lacks accompanying necessities to match the widely differing content and emphasis of each sector. For example, the dissimilarity of the four sectors suggests that faculties can be equally dissimilar and trained according to the needs of their students and the nature of their institution. At present, most colleges and universities seek new hires trained in traditional research-oriented Ph.D. graduate programs, chiefly for prestige purposes. Even some community colleges prefer Ph.D. holders. While a number of today's potential faculty are likely to engage in research and the advancement of knowledge, especially those headed toward the better liberal arts colleges and leading universities and colleges, many will from now on spend much of their scholarly lives primarily as teachers of a broad array of cultural and intellectual achievements, past and current, as authorities in some field such as education, engineering, or business, or as experts in remedial instruction. Thus, the selection of campus instructors should increasingly be done with both eyes on the particular sector of U.S. higher education to which the institution primarily belongs.

Moreover, the content of liberal or general education should be tailored to its college or university, its sector, and its clientele. A single archetype, as promoters such as William Bennett advocate for nearly all of U.S. higher education, is no longer valid in our era of greatly increased access.[6] Two-year colleges, for example, need to concentrate more on reading, writing, basic math and statistics, speech, and the use of computers. Public universities may require two sets of liberal arts courses— one for those in their honors colleges and another for their preprofessional students in, say, business, music, or agriculture. And numerous institutions, public and private, will continue to be homes of hybrid higher learning, with remedial preparation, much teaching for contemporary careers, and limited research and scholarship.

## Accommodate Adult Learners

The swelling growth in numbers of adult students, twenty-five years of age and older, represents a fundamental change in American higher education, and numerous U.S. colleges and universities are already beginning to adjust to this change. Traditionally, American colleges and advanced learning were dedicated largely to teaching younger students, usually preparing them for their first job or a lifetime career. There was often a smattering of older students in the classes, frequently hoping to complete their baccalaureate degrees. But today, adult enrollments may be approaching 35 or 40 percent, and a considerable minority of these adults are students who are already highly educated executives, professionals, and midlevel experts trying to learn more about other cultures, economies, religions, and political systems or about introducing new methods of operation in their fields. In other words, most American institutions of higher education now have dual roles: to educate the young and to teach an enlarging number of older students, too. At present, however, there are no adequate statistics on the number of adult learners.[7] We know only from campus reports that the number of enrollees is increasing. For example, Curtis Rogers, dean of admission at Columbia's School of General Studies, estimates that the number of forty- to sixty-year-old applicants has nearly doubled since 2002.[8]

For these adults, nearly all the structures put in place at the turn of the last century for playful adolescents are unsuitable: semesters, full-time and often tenured research faculty, daytime weekday classes, emphasis on theory and concepts, avoidance of practical problems and their possible solutions, and pressure to earn degrees, not just certificates of competence. The old forms simply cannot serve the new explosion of busy working adults and their educational needs. American higher education is breaking into two quite different realms.

Structurally, this seems to require a separate university for adult continuing education alongside the more drawn-out football-fun-fraternity model with a potpourri of liberal arts courses offered. Two universities on one campus with different purposes, schedules, and faculty might seem peculiar, yet dozens of U.S. colleges and universities are actually drifting into this dual-role structure. But few have had the courage to reorganize their structure or openly acknowledge the full consequences of the emerging dual-structure renovation. The purposes of American universities have multiplied as advanced academic education has become a necessity not only for many young people but also for a burgeoning number of adults who desire to keep up with new developments. A full-fledged, unashamed new layer and kind of higher education—a major structural addition—is imperative. And all its constituent elements ought to be imaginatively designed to serve the new and different adult students.

## Rethink Departments and Disciplines

Another structural renovation must grow out of the gradual change from the ideal of higher education as largely devoted to the dissemination of the world's best knowledge and art and the discovery of new knowledge, especially through research, to a new purpose in society. At present, the academic disciplines control much of this old ideal in U.S. higher education, including the ingredients of liberal education, the major system, the selection and promotion of faculty, the methods of inquiry, and the content of courses. The departmental structure has remained mainly unchanged since 1910 or so and is uniquely American (until the last two decades) and uniquely powerful. As Andrew Abbott says in his discerning essay, "The Disciplines and the Future," "Disciplinary departments are the essential and irreplaceable building blocks of American universities . . . Disciplines in fact provide a core element of the identity of most intellectuals in modern America."[9] And Michael Gibbons observes that, "in disciplinary science, peer review operates to channel individuals toward work on problems judged to be central to the advance of the discipline. These problems are defined largely in terms of criteria which reflect the intellectual interests and pre-occupations of the discipline and its gatekeepers."[10]

But this powerful, many-faceted grip on U.S. higher education by the century-old department structure and its ideal is eroding under the downpour of contemporary developments. One, of course, is the massive increase in enrollments, with most of the newer entrants barely interested in learning about their civilization's intellectual achievements, in developing new knowledge, or in becoming experts in some one discipline. A second development is the coming together of disciplines in order to produce results that matter, as in bioengineering or in the closer ties between politics, economics, and the military. And third, the structure and controls of the aged department structure pose difficulties for colleges and universities eager to modernize, to be more student-oriented, and to become more entrepreneurial and international.

The fourth development is perhaps the most devastating. The very ideal on which the academic disciplines and elite higher education are based, and to which they still cling, is crumbling. U.S. higher education is adopting a new ideal, to be more pragmatic, to serve society more directly, and to be more effective in turning out competent, flexible, and creative workers. The high-minded ideal of pursuing knowledge for its own sake, often in isolated chunks, is no longer the primary function of most institutions. Instead, as Michael Gibbons writes, the new ideal requires a fundamental "shift from discipline-based learning to problem-based learning," with an emphasis on trans- and interdisciplinary instruction.[11]

Naturally, some thirty or forty U.S. universities will retain the old ideal because they will be the primary creators of new knowledge and ideas. But for most of the other thirty-nine hundred or so degree-granting colleges and universities, the instruction will be more practical, the programs more focused on work and the country's manpower needs, and the teaching less theoretical. Much of the research will be more problem-oriented, often with the fiscal help of corporate dollars, and be more applied in nature. The federal government and most state governments are no longer content to spend roughly one-third of a trillion dollars annually on higher education without demanding more useful results. Also, the lofty ideals of von Humboldt or Newman increasingly seem worthless to the third world and developing nations, where the lack of skilled persons is a major handicap and economic growth is essential.

U.S. higher education has already been moving toward greater practical service for their students, their state supporters, and the nation's needs for more and better schoolteachers, more engineers, and persons able to reach out to other economies and cultures. But the full consequences of this change toward more economically useful higher education and research have not yet been grasped. The change means a diminution of "publish or perish" and a vast and comprehensive increase in the importance of teaching. (Currently the federal government provides billions of dollars for research but almost nothing for teaching.) It also requires a transformation of the governance and management of all but the great research universities and a handful of elite liberal arts colleges.[12] The hiring and training of the faculty will also need to be reassessed.

## Revise Cost Structures

Educators need to be more imaginative in finding ways to slow or reduce the alarming rise in costs at U.S. colleges and universities. The College Board estimates that students and their parents borrowed more than $157 billion in loans from the federal government in 2005–2006 and at least another $17 billion from private lenders.

This escalation has become a serious worry for parents, many state legislators, and a small group of in-house economists.[13] Numerous scholars have noted that the escalating tuition and housing costs are "not sustainable." Since 1981, higher education has been the fastest-growing component of the consumer price index, and costs at nearly all institutions show few signs of leveling off. Economist Ronald Ehrenberg, in his excellent book *Tuition Rising: Why College Costs So Much,* details the ingenious attempts to reduce expenditures when he became Cornell University's Vice President for Academic Programs, Planning, and Budgeting in 1995. He paints a vivid picture of how most leading faculty pay little attention to the rising costs of the institution and tend to behave as independent entrepreneurs or henchmen of their disciplines, opposed to greater frugalities at the university.

Higher education's cost cannot be reduced much more through additional incremental cuts. Only major structural redesign can result in significant decreases in costs. Also, U.S. higher education needs to introduce some dramatic alterations, if only to show the American public that academe is sensitive to the mounting indignation toward ever-increasing tuition, fees, and housing costs. The health care field has to some extent restructured to stem escalating costs in services. Higher education should follow with its own rationally chosen renovations.

I think there are at least three structural reforms that could make a difference to parents and anxious legislators, as well as to numerous students.

ONE IS TO REPLACE MANY four-year colleges with three-year undergraduate programs. The reasons are numerous. More students take the advanced placement tests each year, and the tests are now offered at approximately four hundred secondary schools. So a growing minority of college students have achieved sophomore status, or close to it, when they enroll. A higher percentage of college graduates than ever go on to graduate or professional schools, so the necessity for undergraduates to "major" in some subject for depth in a discipline is undercut because graduates will "major" in law, engineering, medicine, business, or some field of graduate study. More than 90 percent of graduates of the most renowned colleges and nearly three-quarters of graduates of solid four-year colleges currently pursue graduate work. And many in the bottom two tiers either feel little need for a major or "major" as undergraduates in fields such as music, education, computer science, or art. The century-old major requirement is now largely an anachronism, though academic departments continue to argue for its maintenance.

A growing number of students now finish in seven semesters. At Johns Hopkins University, for example, more than 20 percent annually complete their degrees at least one semester early. The new information technology allows undergraduates to learn from on-line courses and two-way video conferencing, which makes eight semesters on campus less important. And students are usually older now than they were a century ago. (Charles Eliot, the longtime president of Harvard, entered college at age fifteen and graduated before he was twenty years old.) So students may now require less than four years of college life for grooming. Then, too, the explosion in continuing higher education enables recent college graduates to add a course or two that they might regret not having taken during their three-year stint.

There is also the fact that undergraduate studies in England are three years in length, not four. The same is true for many of the universities in Canada, and in 1999 the members of the European Union (EU), in the "Bologna process," agreed on a common length of undergraduate studies in Europe—three years—to rationalize the disparate time arrangements of different EU countries. In the United States, the three-year baccalaureate is not new, bursting into national attention at Harvard between 1890 and 1910. President Eliot thought college took too long, especially with the advent of sports teams and new extracurricular activities on campus, with five to seven weeks of summer "vacation," the birth of summer schools, and the opening of more graduate programs and professional schools. Between 1896 and 1900, one-sixth of Harvard graduates completed their undergraduate work in three years, and in 1906, 36 percent of the A.B. recipients did so in three years.[14] After World War II, between 1945 and 1950, numerous veterans, with the GI Bill helping, attended summer schools and took extra courses to finish in three years. Many veterans felt that the war had consumed three or four years of their youth, and most had little interest in athletic team participation, singing or drama groups, or fraternities. Many colleges assisted by granting them some academic credit for their military service.

Then, in the early 1990s, two academic presidents decided that private college education was getting too expensive and noticed that the number of undergraduates who graduated in three and one-half years or less was growing. One was S. Frederick Starr of Oberlin College in Ohio, who in his 1990–91 Annual Report advocated that, at least at premier colleges like Oberlin, schools should introduce a three-year A.B. degree so that parents and students could "reduce the cost to students by nearly one-quarter." For those students who need some remedial work, or dedicated athletes, or underprivileged minorities and immigrant youth, some form of preparatory fourth year could be maintained. Two years later, President Gerhard Casper of Stanford University joined Starr and proposed that Stanford consider offering a three-year degree to reduce the rising costs of elite higher education and to slow down the escalating costs of campus financial aid budgets. Casper also believed that the new technology would enable numerous students to complete courses off-campus. Neither the Oberlin nor Stanford faculties were more than lukewarm about the structural change, however.

Today more than fifteen of America's four-year colleges offer a three-year option, including schools such as Bates in Maine and Valparaiso in Indiana, but the reduction continues to be resisted, despite the new conditions of the past three decades and the widespread, swelling rancor toward U.S. college and university leaders, faculty, and trustees for their apparent intransigence. Institutions seem content to pass on the financial burdens to students, who often need to work part-time in college and take out loans to pay for rapidly rising costs. For the 2006–2007 academic year, tuition and fees at public institutions rose 6.3 percent and those at private colleges increased 5.9 percent, both double the nation's inflation rate. The option of three-year degrees seems a no-brainer.

TO HELP REDUCE COSTS to students, to assist with three-year degrees, and to use the often handsome, well-equipped campus facilities more efficiently, a second structural change should be considered. That change is to use the college year-round with a four-semester schedule. This schedule is already in use at colleges such as Dartmouth, and several states (such as Florida) are considering mandating the scheme of all-year use of the state's campuses. The current two-semester academic year is, believe it or not, based on the agricultural cycle of the previous century, when students were often needed to help with spring planting and fall harvesting. Hence, the September to May college calendar. Colleges no longer need to lie fallow for nearly three months a year.

New arrangements would need to be made for the faculty's time off to write, travel, and do research. Semesters could be reduced to twelve weeks, and other innovative steps would have to be taken. But institutions with a four-semester, year-round scheme could increase their revenues and students could reduce their time to degree completion. Moreover, such a change would help diminish two of the public's criticisms of U.S. colleges and universities: that higher education is prodigal and inefficient and that many professors have too soft and pampered a life, with less teaching than ever and a work year of only eight to nine months.

THE THIRD METHOD for reducing consumer costs (and state expenditures) is to reform the big-time sports programs at Division I universities in a radical way. I realize that this is a highly controversial, even explosive, issue, and one that has prompted dozens of books and many dozens of articles urging a profound transformation in the extraordinary growth of commercialism and near-professional recruitment and in the ersatz education of college athletes.

The costs to the 190 or so Division I schools are huge and rising, consuming millions of dollars annually at each of the big-time sports institutions where dollars are needed for academic and financial aid purposes.[15] Only a half-dozen or so Division I universities did not lose money in recent years. And that was because expensive capital improvements are not usually included in the athletic budget but in the university's capital budget. For example, Louisiana State University has spent $15 million to build an academic center just for athletes, as have several other universities devoted to big-time sports. Schools like the University of Southern California and Georgia spend about $1.5 million annually on tutoring and special academic services for their recruited athletes. The NCAA estimates that the Division I universities spend at least $150 million on special academic help for athletes to keep them eligible. The University of Maryland is spending $50.8 million for an expansion of its stadium, and others like Penn State, Tennessee, and Ohio State have also spent millions expanding their stadium seating—for six to eight home games a year. Other Division I universities have constructed new multi-million-dollar basketball arenas or have invested tens of millions to vault into full Division I status, as have Northwestern, Louisville, and Vanderbilt.

The academic situation is unique and bizarre. Nearly all the athletes at Division I schools are recruited regionally by athletic department recruiters, not by admissions officers. They are often housed separately and most do not take regular academic courses. Each athlete has his (or her) total cost of attending the university paid in full with an athletic scholarship, politely called a grant-in-aid, which is good for only one year at a time so that the athletes are in effect employees who are paid so long as they perform in the sport. Fewer than 40 percent of the basketball players ever graduate, and the percentage of football players is only slightly higher. The problem is systemic. There are no decent minor leagues for football and basketball as there are in baseball and hockey, so to become a highly paid professional player in these two sports, athletes need to pass through an institution of higher learning.

Also, most athletic departments are run as associations that are scarcely attached to their universities. Their rules are largely those of the supervisory NCAA, a cartel, not those of the universities, and the athletic departments have their own budgets, which have almost no cost controls and are heavily supported by so-called "booster clubs" composed mainly of nonalumni who regard the university teams, especially football, as vital regional sources of manly pride. The former athletic director and basketball coach at North Carolina State, Jim Valvano, once said: "We are not even really part of the school anymore anyway. I work for the NC State Athletic Association . . . You think the chancellor is going to tell me what to do?"[16]

MOST DIVISION I ATHLETIC DEPARTMENTS are run as separate businesses, with salaries for the coaches equaling those of major corporate executives. Many coaches earn between one and three million dollars a year, especially when their fees for sneaker deals, speaking engagements, country club memberships, and product endorsements are included. The University of Louisville, for instance, recently signed its football coach, Bobby Petrino, to a ten-year, $25 million contract. The NCAA has increased its revenues more than 8,000 percent in the past two decades through deals with major broadcast companies, especially television networks. Its executives now receive very high salaries. Yet, unlike the NFL or NBA, the NCAA pays no income taxes, claiming to be an integral part of the nonprofit, tax-exempt university world. In effect, big-time university sports programs are separate entertainment enterprises largely for the enrichment of their leaders but still pretending to be part of the regular academic university and using amateur student athletes. According to James Duderstadt, the former president of the University of Michigan and one of higher education's most knowing observers,

> Big-time college athletics has little to do with the nature and objectives of the contemporary university. Instead, it is a commercial venture, aimed primarily at providing public entertainment for those beyond the campus and at generating rewards for those who stage it . . . We have allowed those who profit from big-time college sports—celebrity coaches, athletic directors, the sports press, the entertainment industry—to exploit strong and occasionally obsessive public interest to pressure and manipulate the university to their own ends.[17]

The House Ways and Means Committee in 2006 demanded that the NCAA justify how the Division I sports industry, which generates millions of dollars a year and pays huge salaries to its principals, can continue to claim tax-exempt status. The NCAA replied with the usual vague argument that big-time sports are an extension of the higher education enterprise.

Economist Andrew Zimbalist, both a scholar of and consultant to the commercial sports industry, has suggested, as have others, that the Division I universities professionalize their football and basketball teams to end the hypocrisy and drain on university expenses. The players would be paid as minor league players, possibly with subsidies from the professional teams. As separate business entities, the teams would rent the stadiums or arenas and keep all their earnings. They would still be called the Georgia Bulldogs or Michigan Wolverines, so most of the fans might be pleased. But the players would not be forced to masquerade as regular college students, though some might choose to take courses at the campus. The Division I universities would save millions a year. Naturally the highly paid and subsidized coaches and NCAA officials would fiercely oppose such a structural change. But the escalating finances of higher education compel new courageous leadership and an end to the increasingly expensive and embarrassing entertainment businesses that have grown like cancers next to their academic missions.

ONE COULD POINT to other structural and cost-cutting alterations to the American higher education enterprise, such as reducing the number of administrators on most campuses or vastly increasing the training of teachers for the different pedagogical tasks brought on by mass higher education. Even a staunch traditionalist like Stanley Katz, former president of the American Council of Learned Societies, now believes that the recent Carnegie Initiative on the Doctorate has shown that "doctoral education is increasingly disrespectful both of the larger intellectual contours of the disciplines and the needs of future teacher-scholars. The reform of doctoral education may well be the crucial focal point for reforming the future professoriates."[18]

An abundance of studies and books suggest how existing colleges and universities might improve their operations in areas ranging from the assessment of student learning and improvement of diversity to state policies toward higher education and improved models of teaching and learning. These are often useful, but they all presume the century-old structure of higher education; very few take account of the new society that the United States has become since the 1970s. Publications on planning nearly always offer better strategic ways to compete against other rival institutions rather than recommending structural changes to serve the needs of America's emerging new student population, to provide economic and international expertise, and to take full advantage of the radically different communications technologies. And very few analyses offer structural ideas to reduce the escalating costs of college.

This book has tried to suggest that small incremental improvements and better strategic methods and designs may continue to help academe but that the urgent task of higher education's faculty, executives, trustees, and such academic associations as the American Association of University Professors (AAUP), the Association of American Colleges and Universities (AACU), and the Association for the Study of Higher Education (ASHE) is now to help restructure U.S. higher education for the nation's new conditions internally as a society and externally as a competitor in a changing world economy.

# NOTES

---

## Preface

1. William Willimon and Thomas Naylor, *The Abandoned Generation: Rethinking Higher Education* (Grand Rapids, MI: Eerdmans, 1995), 102.

2. William Plater, "Future Work: Faculty Time in the Twenty-first Century," *Change* 27 (May–June 1995): 25.

3. Daniel Cheever Jr., "Tomorrow's Crisis: The Cost of College," *Harvard Magazine* 95 (November–December 1992): 43.

4. William Honan, "New Pressures on the University," Education Life, *New York Times*, January 9, 1994.

5. See, for example, Edwin Slosson, *Great American Universities* (New York: Macmillan, 1910); Frederick Rudolph, *The American College and University: A History* (New York: Knopf, 1962); Laurence Veysey, *The Emergence of the American University* (Chicago: University of Chicago Press, 1965); W. Bruce Leslie, *Gentlemen and Scholars: College and Community in the "Age of the University": 1865–1917* (University Park: Pennsylvania State University Press, 1992); George Marsden and Bradley Longfield, eds., *The Secularization of the Academy* (New York: Oxford University Press, 1992); James Tunstead Burtchaell, *The Dying of the Light: The Disengagement of Colleges and Universities from Their Christian Churches* (Grand Rapids, MI: Eerdmans, 1998).

6. Lawrence Cremin, *Public Education* (New York: Basic Books, 1976).

7. K. Patricia Cross, "The Changing Role of Higher Education in the United States," *Higher Education Research and Development* 6, no. 2 (1987): 102.

## Chapter 1. The Ingredients of the New Society

1. Bernard Bailyn, *Education in the Forming of American Society: Needs and Opportunities for Study* (New York: Norton, 1972).

2. John Dewey, *The School and Society* (New York: McClure, Phillips, 1900).

3. John Dewey, *Democracy and Education* (New York: Macmillan, 1916), 38–39.

4. Daniel Bell, *The Reforming of General Education* (New York: Columbia University Press, 1966); *The Coming of Post-industrial Society: A Venture in Social Forecasting* (New York: Basic Books, 1973); "Teletext and Technology," "The New Class: A Muddled Concept," and "Ethnicity and Social Change," in *The Winding Passage: Essays and Sociological Journeys, 1960–1980* (Cambridge, MA: Abt Books, 1980).

5. James S. Coleman, *The Adolescent Society: The Social Life of the Teenager and Its Impact on Education* (Glencoe, IL: Free Press, 1961); "Families and Schools," *Educational Researcher* 16 (August–September 1987): 32–38; "Social Capital in the Creation of Human Capital," Supplement, *American Journal of Sociology* 94 (1988): S95–120; James S. Coleman and Torsten Husén, *Becoming Adult in a Changing Society* (Paris: Organization for Economic Co-operation and Development, 1985).

6. Richard Hofstadter and Walter Metzger, *The Development of Academic Freedom in the United States* (New York: Columbia University Press, 1955); Richard Hofstadter, *Anti-intellectualism in American Life* (New York: Knopf, 1963).

7. Clark Kerr, *The Uses of the University*, 5th ed. (Cam-

bridge: Harvard University Press, 2001); "Speculations about the Increasingly Indeterminate Future of Higher Education in the United States," *Review of Higher Education* 20 (Summer 1997): 345–56.

8. Christopher Jencks and David Riesman, *The Academic Revolution* (New York: Doubleday, 1968); David Riesman, *On Higher Education* (San Francisco: Jossey-Bass, 1980).

9. Martin Trow, "Reflections on the Transition from Mass to Universal Higher Education," *Daedalus* 99 (Winter 1970): 1–42; "Expansion and Transformation of Higher Education," *International Review of Education* 18 (1972): 61–83; "American Higher Education: Exceptional or Just Different?" in *Is America Different? A New Look at American Exceptionalism,* ed. Byron Shafer (Oxford: Clarendon Press, 1991), 138–86; "Class, Race, and Higher Education in America," *American Behavioral Scientist* 35 (1992): 585–605.

10. See especially James S. Coleman, "The Rational Reconstruction of Society," *American Sociological Review* 58 (February 1993): 9, and "Social Capital in the Creation of Human Capital," Supplement, *American Journal of Sociology* 94 (1988): S95–120.

11. Robert Bellah, Richard Madsen, William Sullivan, Ann Swidler, and Steven Tipton, *Habits of the Heart: Individualism and Commitment in American Life* (Berkeley and Los Angeles: University of California Press, 1985); Charles Taylor, *Sources of the Self* (Cambridge: Harvard University Press, 1989).

12. Vivian Center Seltzer, "Look Who's Coming to College," *Planning for Higher Education* 19 (1991–92): 11–17; Judith Rich Harris, *The Nurture Assumption: Why Children Turn Out the Way They Do* (New York: Free Press, 1998).

13. Peter Drucker, "The Future That Has Already Happened," *Harvard Business Review* 75 (September–October 1997): 20.

14. "6.3 Brides for Seven Brothers," *Economist*, December 19, 1998, 56–58.

15. Samuel Preston, "Children Will Pay," *New York Times Magazine*, September 29, 1996, 96–97. See also Ben Wattenberg, *Fewer: How the New Demography of Depopulation Will Shape Our Future* (Chicago: Ivan Dee, 2004), and Philip Longman, *The Empty Cradle: How Falling Birthrates Threaten World Prosperity and What to Do about It* (New York: Basic Books, 2004).

16. Charles Morris, *The AARP: America's Most Powerful Lobby and the Clash of Generations* (New York: Times Books/ Random House, 1996).

17. Lester Thurow, "The Birth of a Revolutionary Class," *New York Times Magazine*, May 19, 1996, 46–47.

18. Kenneth Young, "Rediscovering the Joy of Learning," *AAHE Bulletin*, December 1996, 7–10.

19. Peter Brimelow, *Alien Nation: Common Sense about America's Immigration Disaster* (New York: Random House, 1995), 76.

20. Roberto Suro, *Strangers among Us: How Latino Immigration Is Transforming America* (New York: Knopf, 1998), 6, 9, 23, 36. See also Nestor Rodriguez, "Globalization, Autonomy, and Transnational Migration," *Research in Policies and Society* 6 (1999): 65–84.

21. George Borjas, *Heaven's Door: Immigration Policy and the American Economy* (Princeton: Princeton University Press, 1999).

22. For instance, Adalberto Aguirre Jr. and Ruben Martinez, *Chicanos in Higher Education: Issues and Dilemmas for the Twenty-first Century*, ASHE-ERIC Higher Education Report 3 (San Francisco: Jossey-Bass/ASHE, 1993).

23. Preston, "Children Will Pay," 97.

24. See, for examples, Irwin Garfinkel and Sara McLanahan, *Single Mothers and Their Children: A New American Dilemma* (Washington, DC: Urban Institute, 1986); Daniel

Patrick Moynihan, *Family and Nation* (San Diego: Harcourt Brace Jovanovich, 1986); Marian Wright Edelman, *Families in Peril: An Agenda for Social Change* (Cambridge: Harvard University Press, 1987); James S. Coleman, "Families and Schools," *Educational Researcher* 16 (1987): 32–38; Sara Levitan, Richard Belous, and Frank Gallo, *What's Happening to the American Family? Tensions, Hopes, Realities* (Baltimore: Johns Hopkins University Press, 1998); David Popenoe, "Family Decline in America," in *Rebuilding the Nest: A New Commitment to the American Family,* ed. David Blankenhorn, Steven Bayme, and Jean Bethke Elshtain (Milwaukee: Family Service America, 1990); Frances Goldschneider and Linda Waite, *New Families, No Families? The Transformation of the American Home* (Berkeley and Los Angeles: University of California Press, 1991); Sara McLanahan and Gary Sandefur, *Growing Up with a Single Parent: What Hurts, What Helps* (Cambridge: Harvard University Press, 1994); Robert Haveman and Barbara Wolfe, *Succeeding Generations: On the Effects of Investment in Children* (New York: Russell Sage Foundation, 1994); David Blankenhorn, *Fatherless America: Confronting Our Most Urgent Social Problem* (New York: Basic Books, 1995); David Popenoe, "A World without Fathers," *Wilson Quarterly* 20 (Spring 1996): 12–28; Susan Mayer, *What Money Can't Buy: Family Income and Children's Life Chances* (Cambridge: Harvard University Press, 1997); Stephanie Coontz, *The Way We Really Are: Coming to Terms with America's Changing Families* (New York: Basic Books, 1997); Nicholas Eberstadt, "Prosperous Paupers and Affluent Savages," *Society* 35 (1998): 393–401; and Dalton Conley and Karen Albright, eds., *After the Bell: Family Background, Public Policy, and Educational Success* (London: Routledge, 2004).

25. For one example, see James Galbraith, *Created Unequal: The Crisis in American Pay* (New York: Free Press, 1998).

26. James Q. Wilson, *On Character* (Washington, DC: AEI Press, 1995).

27. Daniel Patrick Moynihan, "Defining Deviancy Down," *American Scholar* 62 (1993): 17–30.

28. Carnegie Corporation, *Starting Points: Meeting the Needs of Our Youngest Children* (New York: Carnegie Corp., 1994).

29. Lawrence Stone, review of *Putting Asunder: A History of Divorce in Western Society*, by Roderick Phillips, *New York Review of Books*, March 2, 1989, 14.

30. Reynolds Farley, "The Effects of Family Breakdown," *Planning for Higher Education* 24 (1995–96): 60.

31. Chester Finn Jr., *Ten Tentative Truths* (Minneapolis: Center of the American Experiment, 1990).

32. Bellah et al., *Habits of the Heart;* Daniel Yankelovich, *The New Morality: A Profile of American Youth in the 70s* (New York: McGraw-Hill, 1974).

33. James M. Tanner, *Growth at Adolescence* (Oxford: Blackwell, 1962).

34. Peter Berger and Richard John Neuhaus, *To Empower People: The Role of Mediating Structures in Public Policy* (Washington, DC: AEI Press, 1975).

35. Tamar Lewin, "Study Finds that Youngest U.S. Children Are Poorest," *New York Times*, March 15, 1998.

36. Andrew Peyton Thomas, *Crime and the Sacking of America: The Roots of Chaos* (Dulles, VA: Brassey's, 1994).

37. David Popenoe, "A World without Fathers," *Wilson Quarterly* 20 (Spring 1996): 15.

38. David Courtwright, *Violent Land: Single Men and Social Disorder from the Frontier to the Inner City* (Cambridge: Harvard University Press, 1996).

39. Quoted in David Popenoe, *War over the Family* (New Brunswick, NJ: Transaction, 2005), 129.

40. Sara McLanahan and Gary Sandefur, *Growing Up with a Single Parent: What Hurts, What Helps* (Cambridge: Harvard University Press, 1994), 2, 45.

41. Ibid., 48.

42. *Economist,* March 20, 1993, 33.

43. Jean Bethke Elshtain, "The Family and Civic Life," in *Rebuilding the Nest: A New Commitment to the American Family,* ed. David Blankenhorn, Steven Bayme, and Jean Bethke Elshtain (Milwaukee: Family Service America, 1990), 128.

44. Susan Mayer, *What Money Can't Buy: Family Income and Children's Life Chances* (Cambridge: Harvard University Press, 1997), 12.

45. Herbert Walberg, "Families as Partners in Educational Productivity," *Phi Delta Kappan* 65 (February 1984): 397–400.

46. James S. Coleman, "Families and Schools," *Educational Researcher* 16 (August–September 1987): 33.

47. U.S. Commission on Civil Rights, quoted in Philip Lawler, "The New Counterculture," *Wall Street Journal,* August 13, 1993; Elaine Ciulla Kamarck and William Galston, *Putting Children First: A Progressive Family Policy for the 1990s* (Washington, DC: Progressive Policy Institute, September 1990).

48. "The Nature of Poverty," *Wall Street Journal,* March 30, 1995.

49. Michael McPherson and Morton Owen Schapiro, *The Student Aid Game: Meeting Need and Rewarding Talent in American Higher Education* (Princeton: Princeton University Press, 1998), 30, 60.

50. Kenneth Woodward, "Young beyond Their Years," Special Edition on the Twenty-first Century Family, *Newsweek,* Winter–Spring, 1990, 54–60.

51. Arthur Levine and Jana Nidiffer, *Beating the Odds: How the Poor Get to College* (San Francisco: Jossey-Bass, 1996).

52. Alan Charles Kors and Harvey Silvergate, *The Shadow University: The Betrayal of Liberty on America's Campuses* (New York: Free Press, 1998).

53. A vivid description of students' sense of self-pity is

Katie Roiphe's *The Morning After: Sex, Fear, and Feminism on Campus* (Boston: Little, Brown, 1993).

54. Michael Lind, "The Beige and the Black," *New York Times Magazine*, August 16, 1998, 38–39.

55. Lawrence Wright, "One Drop of Blood," *New Yorker*, July 24, 1994, 46–55.

56. Linda Chavez, *Out of the Barrio* (New York: Basic Books, 1991).

57. E. Digby Baltzell, *Philadelphia Gentlemen: The Making of a National Upper Class* (Philadelphia: University of Pennsylvania Press, 1979).

58. Shoshana Zuboff, *In the Age of the Smart Machine: The Future of Work and Power* (New York: Basic Books, 1988).

59. Michael Hammer and Steven Stanton, *The Reengineering Revolution: A Handbook* (New York: HarperCollins, 1995).

60. David Diringer, *The Alphabet: A Key to the History of Mankind*, 2nd ed., rev. (New York: Philosophical Library, 1953).

61. See, for instance, Henry Petroski's remarkable book, *The Pencil: A History of Design and Circumstance* (New York: Knopf, 1990).

62. Walter J. Ong, *Orality and Literacy: The Technologizing of the Word* (London: Routledge, 1988), 82.

63. Lionel Casson, *Libraries in the Ancient World* (New Haven: Yale University Press, 2001).

64. Ong, *Orality and Literacy*, 85.

65. Elizabeth Eisenstein, *The Printing Revolution in Early Modern Europe* (New York: Cambridge University Press, 1983), 12. See also Adrian Johns, *The Nature of the Book: Print and Knowledge in the Making* (Chicago: University of Chicago Press, 1998), and Douglas McMurtrie, *The Book: The Story of Printing and Bookmaking* (New York: Dorset, 1943).

66. Nicholas Negroponte, *Being Digital* (New York: Vintage, 1996), 14–18.

67. Leslie Simon, "Present at the Creation," *Wilson Quarterly* 22 (Autumn 1998): 41–42.

68. Douglas Robertson, *The New Renaissance: Computers and the Next Level of Civilization* (New York: Oxford University Press, 1998), 3, 7.

69. John B. Thompson, *The Media and Modernity: A Social Theory of the Media* (Stanford: Stanford University Press, 1995), 4, 9.

70. Jay David Bolter, *Writing Space: The Computer, Hypertext, and the History of Writing* (Hillsdale, NJ: Lawrence Erlbaum, 1991), 2.

71. Patricia Gumport and Marc Chun, "Technology and Higher Education," in *American Higher Education in the Twenty-first Century: Social, Political, and Economic Challenges,* ed. Philip Altbach, Robert Berdahl, and Patricia Gumport (Baltimore: Johns Hopkins University Press, 1998), 372–73.

72. Brian Hawkins and Patricia Battin, eds., *The Mirage of Continuity: Reconfiguring Academic Information Resources for the Twenty-first Century* (Washington, DC: Council on Library and Information Resources/Association of American Universities, 1998), 6, 10, 261. See also William Arms, *Digital Libraries* (Cambridge: MIT Press, 2000).

73. Robert Samuelson, *The Good Life and Its Discontents: The American Dream in the Age of Entitlement, 1945–1995* (New York: Times Books, 1995); Frank Levy, *The New Dollars and Dreams: American Incomes and Economic Change* (New York: Russell Sage Foundation, 1998).

74. Levy, *New Dollars,* 38.

75. McPherson and Schapiro, *The Student Aid Game,* 28.

76. Chester Finn Jr., *Scholars, Dollars, and Bureaucrats* (Washington, DC: Brookings Institution, 1978), 176.

77. Hugh Davis Graham and Nancy Diamond, *The Rise of American Research Universities: Elites and Challengers in the Postwar Era* (Baltimore: Johns Hopkins University

Press, 1997), 34. See also Bruce L. R. Smith, *American Science Policy since World War II* (Washington, DC: Brookings Institution, 1990), and Roger Geiger, *Research and Relevant Knowledge: American Research Universities since World War II* (New York: Oxford University Press, 1993).

78. Kerr, *The Uses of the University*, v–vi, 87.

79. George Keller, *Academic Strategy: The Management Revolution in American Higher Education* (Baltimore: Johns Hopkins University Press, 1983), 8–14.

80. Bruce Schulman, *The Seventies: The Great Shift in American Culture, Society, and Politics* (New York: Free Press, 2001), xii.

81. David Frum, *How We Got Here: The 70's, The Decade That Brought You Modern Life* (New York: Basic Books, 2000), xxiv.

82. Ibid., 340–43.

83. James Patterson, *Restless Giant: The United States from Watergate to Bush vs. Gore* (New York: Oxford University Press, 2005), 15.

84. Daniel Heath, ed., *America in Perspective: Major Trends in the United States through the 1990s* (Boston: Houghton Mifflin, 1986), 88–90.

85. *New York Times,* January 6, 1982.

86. See the remarkable essay by Tom Wolfe, "The Me Decade and the Third Great Awakening," in his *The Purple Decades* (New York: Berkley Books, 1983), 265–96.

87. Jerry Rubin, *Growing (Up) at 37* (New York: Evans, 1976), 20.

88. Christopher Lasch, *The Culture of Narcissism: American Life in an Age of Diminishing Expectations* (New York: Norton, 1978), 235.

89. Gregg Easterbrook, *The Progress Paradox: How Life Gets Better While People Feel Worse* (New York: Random House, 2003), 107–8.

90. Terry Anderson, *The Pursuit of Fairness: A History*

*of Affirmative Action* (New York: Oxford University Press, 2004); Hugh Davis Graham, *Collision Course: The Strange Convergence of Affirmative Action and Immigration Policy in America* (New York: Oxford University Press, 2002).

91. John Zysman and Stephen Cohen, "The International Experience," in *The Changing American Economy,* ed. David Obey and Paul Sarbanes (New York: Basil Blackwell, 1986), 41–42.

92. Timothy Taylor, "The Truth about Globalization," *Public Interest* 147 (Spring 2002): 26.

93. Daniel Bell, "Liberalism in the Postindustrial Society," in *The Winding Passage: Essays and Sociological Journeys, 1960–1980* (Cambridge, MA: Abt Books, 1980), 238.

94. Stephen Barley and Julian Orr, eds., *Between Craft and Science: Technical Work in U.S. Settings* (Ithaca: Cornell University Press, 1997), 7, 41.

95. Robert William Fogel, *The Fourth Great Awakening and the Future of Egalitarianism* (Chicago: University of Chicago Press, 2000), 219.

96. See, as examples, Michael Porter, *Competitive Strategy* (New York: Free Press, 1980), and Gary Hamel and C. K. Prahalad, *Competing for the Future* (Boston: Harvard Business School Press, 1994).

97. J. H. Plumb, *The Death of the Past* (Boston: Houghton Mifflin, 1970), 14.

98. Philip Jenkins, *Decade of Nightmares: The End of the Sixties and the Making of Eighties America* (New York: Oxford University Press, 2006), 183.

99. See, for instance, Renato Ruggiero, "The High Stakes of World Trade," *Wall Street Journal,* April 28, 1997.

100. Walter Powell and Jason Owen-Smith, "The New World of Knowledge Production in the Life Sciences," in *The Future of the City of Intellect: The Changing American University,* ed. Steven Brint (Stanford: Stanford University Press, 2002), 107–30.

101. Michael Young, *The Rise of the Meritocracy, 1870–2033: The New Elite of Our Social Revolution* (New York: Random House, 1959), 12, 59.

102. Finis Welch, ed., *The Causes and Consequences of Increasing Inequality* (Chicago: University of Chicago Press, 2001), 4.

103. Mickey Kaus, *The End of Equality* (New York: Basic Books, 1992), 31.

104. See, for example, Steven Brint, "The Rise of the 'Practical Arts,'" in Brint, *The Future of the City of Intellect*, 231–59.

105. Christopher Lasch, *The New Radicalism in America, 1889–1963: The Intellectual as a Social Type* (New York: Knopf, 1965), 316.

106. Robert Frank and Philip Cook, *The Winner-Take-All Society* (New York: Free Press, 1995), 13.

107. *Chronicle of Higher Education*, November 18, 2005, Section B.

108. Frank and Cook, *The Winner-Take-All Society*, 147–66.

109. George Keller, "The Emerging Third Stage in Higher Education Planning," *Planning for Higher Education* 28 (Winter 1999–2000), 1–7.

110. Alexis de Tocqueville, *Democracy in America* (1835; repr., New York: Vintage, 1945), 1:3.

111. Ronald Mincy, *Black Males Left Behind* (Washington, DC: Urban Institute Press, 2006). See also Orlando Patterson, "A Poverty of the Mind," *New York Times*, March 26, 2006.

112. Frum, *How We Got Here*, 250.

113. *Chronicle of Higher Education*, December 3, 2004, A11.

114. Bell, "The New Class," 161.

115. See, for instance, John Skrentny, *The Minority Rights Revolution* (Cambridge: Harvard University Press, 2002).

116. Richard Herrnstein, "IQ," *Atlantic Monthly*, September 1971, 43–64.

117. Young, *The Rise of the Meritocracy*, 87.

118. Charles Murray, "IQ, Success, and Inequality: The Ambiguous Merits of Meritocracy," in Welch, *The Causes and Consequences*, 334.

## Chapter 2. Education's Response to the New Society

1. Ernest Boyer, *College: The Undergraduate Experience in America* (New York: Harper & Row, 1987), 242. See also, among others, Martin Trow, "The Academic Senate as a School for University Leadership," in *Liberal Education* 76 (January–February 1990): 23–27; Joanna Scott, "Death by Inattention: The Strange Fate of Faculty Governance," *Academe* 83 (November–December 1997): 28–33; and William Tierney, ed., *Competing Conceptions of Academic Governance: Negotiating the Perfect Storm* (Baltimore: Johns Hopkins University Press, 2004).

2. K. Patricia Cross, *Adults as Learners: Increasing Participation and Facilitating Learning* (San Francisco: Jossey-Bass, 1981); Jerold Apps, *Higher Education in a Learning Society: Meeting New Demands for Education and Training* (San Francisco: Jossey-Bass, 1988).

3. Ben Gose, "Surge in Continuing Education Brings Profits for Universities," *Chronicle of Higher Education*, February 19, 1999, A51–52.

4. Two excellent descriptions of the new postsecondary programs for adults are Theodore Marchese, "Not-So-Distant Competitors: How New Providers Are Remaking the Post-Secondary Marketplace," *AAHE Bulletin*, May 1998, 3–7, and Alice Irby, "Post-Baccalaureate Certificates," *Change* 31 (March–April 1999): 36–43. See also Kay Kohl and Jules LaPidus, eds., *Postbaccalaureate Futures: New Markets, Resources, Credentials* (Phoenix, AZ: ACE/Oryx, 2000).

5. Thomas Sowell, *Migrations and Cultures* (New York: Basic Books, 1996); Lawrence Harrison and Samuel Hunt-

ington, eds., *Culture Matters: How Values Shape Human Progress* (New York: Basic Books, 2000).

6. Orlando Patterson, "Is Affirmative Action on the Way Out?" *Commentary,* March 1998, 45. See also Hugh Davis Graham, *Collision Course: The Strange Convergence of Affirmative Action and Immigration Policy in America* (New York: Oxford University Press, 2002). Graham argues that immigration poses a major threat to existing civil rights policy.

7. Corynne McSherry, *Who Owns Academic Work? Battling for Control of Intellectual Property* (Cambridge: Harvard University Press, 2001).

8. Quotations from John Seely Brown and Paul Duguid, "Universities in the Digital Age," in *The Mirage of Continuity: Reconfiguring American Information Resources for the Twenty-first Century,* ed. Brian Hawkins and Patricia Battin (Washington, DC: Council on Library and Information Resources/Association of American Universities, 1998), 44, 54; Brown and Duguid, *The Social Life of Information* (Boston: Harvard Business School Press, 2000), 128; Brown and Duguid, "Universities in the Digital Age," 45; Brown and Duguid, *The Social Life of Information,* 219, 121, 61. See also John Seely Brown, "Growing Up Digital: How the Web Changes Work, Education, and the Ways People Learn," *Change* 32 (March–April 2000): 11–20.

9. Jack Schuster and Martin Finkelstein, *The American Faculty: The Restructuring of Academic Work and Careers* (Baltimore: Johns Hopkins University Press, 2006), 333. See also Martin Finkelstein, Carol Frances, Frank Jewett, and Bernhard Scholz, eds., *Dollars, Distance, and Online Education: The New Economics of College Teaching and Learning* (Phoenix, AZ: ACE/Oryx Press, 2000).

10. William Baumol and Sue Anne Batey Blackman, "How To Think about Rising College Costs," *Planning for Higher Education* 23 (Summer 1995): 1–7.

11. James Duderstadt, *Intercollegiate Athletics and the Amer-*

*ican University: A University President's Perspective* (Ann Arbor: University of Michigan Press, 2000); Andrew Zimbalist, *Unpaid Professionals: Commercialism and Conflict in Big-Time College Sports* (Princeton: Princeton University Press, 2001); Murray Sperber, *College Sports, Inc.: The Athletic Department vs. the University* (New York: Holt, 1990).

12. Schuster and Finkelstein, *The American Faculty*; Judith Gappa and David Leslie, *The Invisible Faculty: Improving the Status of Part-Timers in Higher Education* (San Francisco: Jossey-Bass, 1999). See also the brilliant article by Martin Finkelstein, "The Morphing of the Academic Profession," *Liberal Education* 89 (Fall 2003): 6–15.

13. Robert Clark and P. Brett Hammond, eds., *To Retire or Not? Retirement Policy and Practice in Higher Education* (Philadelphia: University of Pennsylvania Press, 2001).

14. Alan Wolfe, "The New Class Comes Home," in *Our Country, Our Culture: The Politics of Political Correctness,* ed. Edith Kurzweil and William Phillips (Boston: Partisan Review Press, 1994), 283. There are at least a half dozen good books and numerous articles describing the growing politicalization at many colleges and universities. The Kurzweil and Phillips volume of collected essays, I have found, is among the best.

15. Steven Marcus, "Soft Totalitarianism," in Kurzweil and Phillips, *Our Country, Our Culture*, 161.

16. John Searle, "Is There a Crisis in American Higher Education?" in Kurzweil and Phillips, *Our Country, Our Culture,* 232.

## Chapter 3. What's Next for America's Colleges and Universities?

1. For a detailed account of how one college changed appreciably since the 1970s, see George Keller, *Prologue to Prominence: A Half Century at Roanoke College* (Minneapolis, MN: Lutheran University Press, 2005).

2. Look, for example, at Sarah Hammond Creighton's *Greening the Ivory Tower: Improving the Environmental Track Record of Universities, Colleges, and Other Institutions* (Cambridge: MIT Press, 1998).

3. Laurence Veysey, "Stability and Experiment in the American Undergraduate Curriculum," in *Content and Context: Essays on College Education,* ed. Carl Kaysen (New York: McGraw-Hill, 1973), 1, 3.

4. See Earl Cheit, *The Useful Arts and the Liberal Tradition* (New York: McGraw-Hill, 1975).

5. Merle Curti and Roderick Nash, *Philanthropy in the Shaping of American Higher Education* (New Brunswick, NJ: Rutgers University Press, 1965).

6. Jesse Sears, *Philanthropy in the History of American Higher Education* (Washington, DC: U.S. Government Printing Office, 1922), 55.

7. Aristotle, *Politics,* trans. Ernest Barker, bk. 8, chap. 2 (Oxford: Clarendon Press, 1948), 392.

8. See, for example, the piercing description of Harvard College's sham of a liberal education in Ross Douthat's "Approaches to Knowledge," chap. 4 in *Privilege: Harvard and the Education of the Ruling Class* (New York: Hyperion, 2005), 111–40, and the lament of Harry Lewis, former dean of Harvard College, in his *Excellence without a Soul: How a Great University Forgot Education* (New York: Public Affairs Press, 2006).

9. Martin Trow, "Admissions and the Crisis in American Higher Education," in *Higher Education for Everybody? Issues and Implications,* ed. W. Todd Furniss (Washington, DC: American Council on Education, 1971), 28, 45.

10. Bernard Shapiro and Harold Shapiro, "Universities in Higher Education: Some Problems and Challenges in a Changing World" (unpublished paper, October 1994).

11. See Michael Gibbons's paper, "Higher Education Relevance in the Twenty-first Century," for the UNESCO

World Conference on Higher Education, Paris, October 5–9, 1998.

12. Jack Schuster and Martin Finkelstein, *The American Faculty: The Restructuring of Academic Work and Careers* (Baltimore: Johns Hopkins University Press, 2006), 3.

13. Gary Hamel and C. K. Prahalad, *Competing for the Future* (Boston: Harvard Business School Press, 1994), x, xi, 308.

14. "The Brains Business: A Survey of Higher Education," *Economist,* September 10, 2005, 3–22.

15. George Keller, "Higher Education Management: Challenges and Strategies," in *International Handbook of Higher Education,* eds. James Forest and Philip Altbach (Dordrecht, Netherlands: Springer, 2006), 229–42.

16. Gibbons, "Higher Education Relevance," 13.

17. Kay Kohl, "The Postbaccalaureate Learning Imperative," in *Postbaccalaureate Futures: New Markets, Resources, Credentials,* ed. Kay Kohl and Jules LaPidus (Phoenix, AZ: ACE/Oryx, 2000), 28.

18. Gibbons, "Higher Education Relevance," 1.

19. Walter Powell and Jason Owen-Smith, "The New World of Knowledge Production in the Life Sciences," in *The Future of the City of Intellect: The Changing American University,* ed. Steven Brint (Stanford: Stanford University Press, 2002), 107–30.

20. Lynnley Browning, "BMW's Custom-Made University," *New York Times,* August 29, 2006.

21. Steven Brint, "The Rise of the 'Practical Arts,'" in *The Future of the City of Intellect,* 253.

22. Ronald Ehrenberg, *Tuition Rising: Why College Costs So Much* (Cambridge: Harvard University Press, 2000), 185.

23. See, for example, Mark Meredith's outstanding *The Fate of Africa* (New York: Public Affairs Press, 2005).

24. Bernard Lewis, *What Went Wrong? The Clash between Islam and Modernity in the Middle East* (New York: Perennial, 2003).

## Chapter 4. Remodeling the Kingpin

1. But see William Henry III, *In Defense of Elitism* (New York: Doubleday, 1994).

2. Read, for example, Francis Oakley, *Community of Learning: The American College and the Liberal Arts Tradition* (New York: Oxford University Press, 1992), and Steven Koblik and Stephen Graubard, eds., *Distinctively American: The Residential Liberal Arts Colleges* (New Brunswick, NJ: Transaction, 2000).

3. W. Bruce Leslie, *Gentlemen and Scholars: College and Community in the "Age of the University," 1865–1917* (New Brunswick, NJ: Transaction, 2005), 258.

4. E. H. Wilkins, *The Changing College* (Chicago: University of Chicago Press, 1927), 75.

5. W. Norton Grubb & Associates, *Honored but Invisible: An Inside Look at Teaching in Community Colleges* (New York: Routledge, 1999).

6. Liberal arts programs are a shambles at research universities from Princeton and Harvard to Stanford and Berkeley; Columbia remains a notable exception. But see the captivating experiments to modernize liberal learning in the liberal arts sector in Michael Nelson and Associates, *Alive at the Core: Exemplary Approaches to General Education in the Humanities* (San Francisco: Jossey-Bass, 2000).

7. See Clifford Adelman, "The Propaganda of Numbers," *Chronicle of Higher Education,* October 13, 2006, B6–9.

8. Catherine Fredman, "Jump Start Your Brain," *New York Times,* October 15, 2006.

9. Andrew Abbott, "The Disciplines and the Future," in *The Future of the City of Intellect: The Changing American University,* ed. Steven Brint (Stanford: Stanford University Press, 2002), 210.

10. Michael Gibbons, "Higher Education Relevance in the Twenty-first Century" (paper presented at the UNESCO

World Conference on Higher Education, Paris, October 5–9, 1998), 9.

11. Ibid., 40.

12. See the chapters by David Collis, James Duderstadt, and George Keller in *Competing Conceptions of Academic Governance: Negotiating the Perfect Storm,* ed. William Tierney (Baltimore: Johns Hopkins University Press, 2004).

13. Ronald Ehrenberg, *Tuition Rising: Why College Costs So Much* (Cambridge: Harvard University Press, 2000); Richard Vedder, *Going Broke by Degree: Why College Costs Too Much* (Washington, DC: AEI Press, 2004).

14. Hugh Hawkins, *Between Harvard and America: The Educational Leadership of Charles W. Eliot* (New York: Oxford University Press, 1972), 116–18.

15. There has been an abundance of data-rich books on big-time university athletics. An eye-opening place to begin is Murray Sperber's *College Sports Inc.: The Athletic Department vs. the University* (New York: Holt, 1990). Other informative books include Rick Telander, *The Hundred Yard Lie: The Corruption of College Football and What We Can Do to Stop It* (New York: Simon & Schuster, 1989); John Thelin, *Games Colleges Play: Scandal and Reform in Intercollegiate Athletics* (Baltimore: Johns Hopkins University Press, 1994); Andrew Zimbalist, *Unpaid Professionals: Commercialism and Conflict in Big-Time College Sports* (Princeton, NJ: Princeton University Press, 2001); and James Duderstadt, *Intercollegiate Athletics and the American University* (Ann Arbor: University of Michigan Press, 2000).

16. Jim Valvano, quoted in Sperber, *College Sports,* 18.

17. Duderstadt, *Intercollegiate Athletics,* 11, 267.

18. Stanley Katz, "What Has Happened to the Professoriate?" *Chronicle of Higher Education,* October 6, 2006, B10.

# SELECTED BIBLIOGRAPHY

Aaron, Henry, Thomas Mann, and Timothy Taylor, eds. *Values and Public Policy.* Washington, DC: Brookings Institution, 1994.

Aguirre, Adalberto, Jr., and Ruben Martinez. *Chicanos in Higher Education: Issues and Dilemmas of the Twenty-first Century.* ASHE-ERIC Higher Education Report 3. San Francisco: Jossey-Bass/ASHE, 1993.

Akerlof, George, and Rachel Kranton. "Identity and Schooling: Some Lessons for the Economics of Education." *Journal of Economic Literature* 40 (December 2002): 1167–1201.

Altbach, Philip, Robert Berdahl, and Patricia Gumport, eds. *American Higher Education in the Twenty-first Century: Social, Political, and Economic Challenges,* 2nd ed. Baltimore: Johns Hopkins University Press, 2005.

Altbach, Philip, Patricia Gumport, and D. Bruce Johnstone, eds. *In Defense of American Higher Education.* Baltimore: Johns Hopkins University Press, 2001.

Amaral, Alberto, Glen A. Jones, and Berit Karseth, eds. *Governing Higher Education: National Perspectives on Institutional Governance.* Dordrecht, Netherlands: Kluwer Academic Publishers, 2002.

Amaral, Alberto, V. Lynn Meek, and Ingvild Larsen, eds. *The Higher Education Managerial Revolution?* Dordrecht, Netherlands: Kluwer Academic Publishers, 2003.

Appiah, K. Anthony. "The Multiculturalist Misunderstanding." Review of *On Toleration*, by Michael Walzer, and of *We Are All Multiculturalists Now*, by Nathan Glazer. *New York Review of Books*, October 9, 1997, 32–33.

Astin, Alexander. *Achieving Academic Excellence*. San Francisco: Jossey-Bass, 1985.

———. *What Matters in College? Four Critical Years Revisited*. San Francisco: Jossey-Bass, 1993.

Astin, Alexander, et al. *The American Freshman: National Norms*. Los Angeles: Higher Education Research Institute, UCLA, published annually.

Bailyn, Bernard. *Education in the Forming of American Society: Needs and Opportunities for Study*. Chapel Hill: University of North Carolina Press, 1960. New York: Norton, 1972.

Balderston, Frederick. *Managing Today's University*. 2nd ed. San Francisco: Jossey-Bass, 1995.

Baldwin, Roger, and Jay Chronister. *Teaching without Tenure: Policies and Practices for a New Era*. Baltimore: Johns Hopkins University Press, 2002.

Barley, Stephen, and Julian Orr, eds. *Between Craft and Science: Technical Work in U.S. Settings*. Ithaca: Cornell University Press, 1997.

Bates, A. W. *Managing Technological Change: Strategies for College and University Leaders*. San Francisco: Jossey-Bass, 2000.

Baumol, William, and Sue Anne Batey Blackman. "How to Think about Rising College Costs." *Planning for Higher Education* 23 (Summer 1995): 1–7.

Becher, Tony, and Paul Trowler. *Academic Tribes and Territories*. Buckingham, UK: Open University Press, 2001.

Bell, Daniel. *The Coming of Post-industrial Society: A Venture in Social Forecasting*. New York: Basic Books, 1973. Special 25th anniversary edition with a new foreword by the author. New York: Basic Books, 1999.

———. *The Reforming of General Education.* New York: Columbia University Press, 1966.

———. *The Winding Passage: Essays and Sociological Journeys, 1960–1980.* Cambridge, MA: Abt Books, 1980. See esp. "The New Class: A Muddled Concept," 144–64.

Bellah, Robert, Richard Madsen, William Sullivan, Ann Swidler, and Steven Tipton. *Habits of the Heart: Individualism and Commitment in American Life.* Berkeley and Los Angeles: University of California Press, 1985.

Ben-David, Joseph. *Centers of Learning: Britain, France, Germany, and the United States.* New York: McGraw-Hill, 1977. Reprint, New Brunswick, NJ: Transaction, 1992.

Bender, Thomas. *Intellect and Public Life: Essays on the Social History of Academic Intellectuals in the United States.* Baltimore: Johns Hopkins University Press, 1993.

Bender, Thomas, and Carl Schorske. *American Academic Culture in Transition.* Princeton: Princeton University Press, 1997.

Benjamin, Roger. "The Environment of Higher Education: A Constellation of Changes." *Annals of the American Academy of Political and Social Science* 585 (January 2003): 8–30.

Benne, Robert. *Quality with Soul: How Six Premier Colleges and Universities Keep Faith with Their Religious Traditions.* Grand Rapids, MI: Eerdmans, 2001.

Berlin, Isaiah. *Against the Current: Essays in the History of Ideas.* Edited by Henry Hardy. New York: Viking, 1980. See esp. "The Divorce between the Sciences and Humanities," 80–110. Also in *The Proper Study of Mankind: An Anthology of Essays.* Edited by Henry Hardy and Roger Hausheer. New York: Farrar, Straus, 1998.

Bernstein, Richard. *Dictatorship of Virtue: Multiculturalism and the Battle for America's Future.* New York: Knopf, 1994.

Birnbaum, Robert. *How Academic Leadership Works.* San Francisco: Jossey-Bass, 1992.

Bok, Derek. *The Cost of Talent: How Executives and Professionals Are Paid and How It Affects America*. New York: Free Press, 1993.

———. *Universities in the Marketplace: The Commercialization of Higher Education*. Princeton: Princeton University Press, 2003.

Borjas, George. *Heaven's Door: Immigration Policy and the American Economy*. Princeton: Princeton University Press, 1999.

Bowen, Howard. *Investment in Learning: The Individual and Social Value of American Higher Education*. San Francisco: Jossey-Bass, 1977. Reprint, Baltimore: Johns Hopkins University Press, 1997.

Bowen, William, and Harold Shapiro, eds. *Universities and Their Leadership*. Princeton: Princeton University Press, 1998.

Boxer, Marilyn Jacoby. *When Women Ask the Questions: Creating Women's Studies in America*. Baltimore: Johns Hopkins University Press, 1998.

Boyer, Ernest. *Scholarship Reconsidered*. Princeton, NJ: Carnegie Foundation for the Advancement of Teaching, 1990.

"The Brains Business." A Survey of Higher Education. *Economist*, September 10, 2005, 3–22.

Breneman, David. *Alternatives to Tenure for the Next Generation of Academics*. Working Paper 14. Washington, DC: American Association for Higher Education, 1997.

———. *Higher Education: On a Collision Course with New Realities*. Occasional Paper 22. Washington, DC: Association of Governing Boards, 1994.

———. *Liberal Arts Colleges: Thriving, Surviving, or Endangered?* Washington, DC: Brookings Institution, 1994.

Brewer, Dominic, Susan Gates, and Charles Goldman. *In Pursuit of Prestige: Strategy and Competition in U.S. Higher Education*. New Brunswick, NJ: Transaction, 2002.

Brint, Steven, ed. *The Future of the City of Intellect: The Changing American University.* Stanford: Stanford University Press, 2002.

Brown, John Seely, and Paul Duguid. *The Social Life of Information.* Boston: Harvard Business School Press, 2000.

———. "Universities in the Digital Age." In *The Mirage of Continuity: Reconfiguring Academic Information Resources for the Twenty-first Century,* edited by Brian Hawkins and Patricia Battin, 39–60. Washington, DC: Council on Library and Information Resources/Association of American Universities, 1998.

Bruner, Jerome. *The Culture of Education.* Cambridge: Harvard University Press, 1996.

Burke, Joseph, ed. *Achieving Accountability in Higher Education.* San Francisco: Jossey-Bass, 2005.

Burness, John. "Mixed (Up) Messages: Universities and the Media." *Gannett Center Journal* 5 (Spring–Summer 1991): 1–15.

Butin, Dan. "The Limits of Service-Learning." *Review of Higher Education* 29 (Summer 2006): 473–98.

Butterfield, Barbara, with Susan Wolfe. *You Can Get There from Here: The Road to Downsizing in Higher Education.* Washington, DC: College and University Personnel Association, 1994.

Cartter, Allan. "Economics of the University." *American Economic Review* 55 (May 1965): 481–94.

Castells, Manuel. *The Information Age: Economy, Society, and Culture.* 3 vols. Oxford: Blackwell, 1996–98.

Chaffee, Ellen. "Successful Strategic Management in Small Private Colleges." *Journal of Higher Education* 55 (1984): 212–41.

Chait, Richard, ed. *The Questions of Tenure.* Cambridge: Harvard University Press, 2002.

Chait, Richard, Thomas Holland, and Barbara Taylor.

*Improving the Performance of Governing Boards.* Phoenix, AZ: ACE/Oryx, 1996.

Clark, Burton. "Collegial Entrepreneurialism in Proactive Universities: Lessons from Europe." *Change* 32 (January–February 2000): 10–19.

———. "Small Worlds, Different Worlds." *Daedalus* 126 (Fall 1997): 21–42.

———. *Sustaining Change in Universities.* Maidenhead, UK: Society for Research into Higher Education/Open University Press, 2004.

Clotfelter, Charles. *Buying the Best: Cost Escalation in Elite Higher Education.* Princeton: Princeton University Press, 1996.

Clotfelter, Charles, and Thomas Ehrlich, eds. *Philanthropy and the Nonprofit Sector in a Changing America.* Bloomington: Indiana University Press, 1999.

Clotfelter, Charles, and Michael Rothschild, eds. *Studies of Supply and Demand in Higher Education.* Chicago: University of Chicago Press, 1993.

Cohen, Arthur. *The Shaping of American Higher Education: Emergence and Growth of the Contemporary System.* San Francisco: Jossey-Bass, 1998.

Cole, Jonathan, Elinor Barber, and Stephen Graubard. *The Research University in a Time of Discontent.* Baltimore: Johns Hopkins University Press, 1994.

Coleman, James S. *The Adolescent Society: The Social Life of the Teenager and Its Impact on Education.* Glencoe, IL: Free Press, 1961.

———. "Families and Schools." *Educational Researcher* 16 (August–September 1987): 32–38.

———. "Social Capital in the Creation of Human Capital." Supplement, *American Journal of Sociology* 94 (1988): S95–120.

———. "The University and Society's New Demands upon It." In *Content and Context: Essays on College Education,* edited by Carl Kaysen, 359–99. New York: McGraw-Hill, 1973.

Coleman, James S., and Torsten Husén. *Becoming Adult in a Changing Society*. Paris: Organization for Economic Co-operation and Development, 1985.

Collis, David. "When Industries Change: The Future of Higher Education." *Continuing Higher Education Review* 65 (2001): 7–24.

Commission on the Academic Presidency. *Renewing the Academic Presidency: Stronger Leadership for Tougher Times*. Washington, DC: Association of Governing Boards of Universities and Colleges, 1996.

Conley, Dalton, and Karen Albright, eds. *After the Bell: Family Background and Educational Success*. London: Routledge, 2004.

Cook, Philip, and Robert Frank. "The Growing Concentration of Top Students at Elite Schools." In *Studies of Supply and Demand in Higher Education,* edited by Charles Clotfelter and Michael Rothschild, 121–144. Chicago: University of Chicago Press, 1993.

Cox, W. Michael, and Richard Alm. *Myths of Rich and Poor*. New York: Basic Books, 1999.

Crainer, Stuart, and Des Dearlove. *Gravy Training: Inside the Business of Business Schools*. San Francisco: Jossey-Bass, 1999.

Cremin, Lawrence. *Popular Education and Its Discontents*. New York: Harper & Row, 1990.

Cross, K. Patricia. "The Changing Role of Higher Education in the United States." *Higher Education Research and Development* 6, no. 2 (1987): 99–108.

Cuban, Larry. *How Scholars Trumped Teachers: Change without Reform in University Curriculum Teaching and Research, 1890–1990*. New York: Teachers College Press, 1999.

Damasio, Antonio. *Descartes' Error: Emotion, Reason, and the Human Brain*. New York: Putnam, 1984.

David, Peter. "Inside the Knowledge Factory." *Economist,* October 4, 1997, 3–22.

Day, Jennifer, and Eric Neuberger. "The Big Payoff: Educational Attainment and Synthetic Estimates of Work-Life Earnings." *Current Population Reports.* Washington, DC: U.S. Census Bureau, July 2002.

Dewey, John. *Democracy and Education.* New York: Macmillan, 1916.

———. *The School and Society.* New York: McClure, Phillips, 1900.

Diamond, Robert. *The Disciplines Speak: Rewarding the Scholarly, Professional and Creative Work of Faculty.* Washington, DC: American Association for Higher Education, 1995.

Dickman, Howard, ed. *The Imperiled Academy.* New Brunswick, NJ: Transaction, 1993.

Dill, David, and Barbara Sporn, eds. *Emerging Patterns of Social Demand and University Reform.* Tarrytown, NY: Elsevier, 1995.

Dovre, Paul, ed. *The Future of Religious Colleges.* Grand Rapids, MI: Eerdmans, 2002.

Dreyfus, Hubert, and Stuart Dreyfus. *Mind over Machine: The Power of Intuition and Expertise in the Era of the Computer.* New York: Free Press, 1986.

Dror, Yehezkel. "Muddling Through—Science or Inertia?" In *Ventures in the Policy Sciences: Concepts and Applications,* 257–63. Tarrytown, NY: Elsevier, 1971.

Drucker, Peter. *The Age of Discontinuity: Guidelines to Our Changing Society.* New York: Harper & Row, 1969.

———. *Innovation and Entrepreneurship.* New York: Harper & Row, 1985.

D'Souza, Dinesh. *Illiberal Education: The Politics of Race and Sex on Campus.* New York: Free Press, 1991.

Duderstadt, James. "Academic Renewal at Michigan." In *Revitalizing Higher Education,* edited by Joel Meyerson and William Massy, 5–18. Princeton, NJ: Peterson's, 1995. Also in *Executive Strategies* 1, 1995.

———. *Intercollegiate Athletics and the American University: A University President's Perspective.* Ann Arbor: University of Michigan Press, 2000.

———. *A University for the Twenty-first Century.* Ann Arbor: University of Michigan Press, 2000.

Easterbrook, Gregg. *A Moment on Earth: The Coming Age of Environmental Optimism.* New York: Viking, 1995.

———. *The Progress Paradox: How Life Gets Better While People Feel Worse.* New York: Random House, 2003.

Eble, Kenneth. *The Art of Administration.* San Francisco: Jossey-Bass, 1978.

Eckel, Peter, and Adrianna Kezar. *Taking the Reins: Institutional Transformation in Higher Education.* Westport, CT: ACE/Praeger, 2003.

Ehrenberg, Ronald. *Tuition Rising: Why College Costs So Much.* Cambridge: Harvard University Press, 2000.

Ehrmann, Stephen. "Beyond Computer Literacy: Implications of Technology for the Content of a College Education." *Liberal Education* 90 (Fall 2004): 6–13.

Epstein, Jason. "The Rattle of Pebbles." *New York Review of Books,* April 27, 2000, 55–59.

Etzkowitz, Henry, Andrew Webster, and Peter Healey, eds. *Capitalizing Knowledge: New Intersections of Industry and Academia.* Albany: State University of New York Press, 1998.

*Facing Change: Building the Faculty of the Future.* Washington, DC: American Association of State Colleges and Universities, 1999.

Finkelstein, Martin. "The Morphing of the American Academic Profession." *Liberal Education* 89 (Fall 2003): 6–15.

Finkelstein, Martin, Robert Seal, and Jack Schuster. *The New Academic Generation: A Profession in Transformation.* Baltimore: Johns Hopkins University Press, 1998.

Finn, Chester, Jr., and Bruce Manno. "Behind the Curtain: What's Wrong with the American University?" *Wilson Quarterly* 20 (Winter 1996): 44–53.

Fisher, James, and James Koch. *Presidential Leadership.* Phoenix, AZ: ACE/Oryx, 1996.

Fiske, Edward, and Bruce Hammond. "Identifying Quality in American Colleges and Universities." *Planning for Higher Education* 26 (Fall 1997): 8–13.

Florida, Richard. *The Rise of the Creative Class.* New York: Basic Books, 2002.

Fogel, Robert William. *The Fourth Great Awakening and the Future of Egalitarianism.* Chicago: University of Chicago Press, 2000.

Frank, Robert, and Philip Cook. *The Winner-Take-All Society.* New York: Free Press, 1995.

Freeland, Richard. "How Practical Experience Can Help Revitalize Our Tired Model of Undergraduate Education." *Chronicle of Higher Education,* February 19, 1999, B6–7.

Friedman, Thomas. *The World Is Flat: A Brief History of the Twenty-first Century.* New York: Farrar, Straus, 2005.

Frum, David. *How We Got Here: The 70s, the Decade That Brought You Modern Life.* New York: Basic Books, 2000.

Fulton, Oliver. "Unity or Fragmentation, Convergence or Diversity: The Academic Profession in Comparative Perspective in the Era of Mass Higher Education." In *Universities and Their Leadership,* edited by William Bowen and Harold Shapiro, 173–96. Princeton: Princeton University Press, 1998.

Gaither, Gerald, ed. *Multicampus System: Perspectives on Practice and Prospects.* Sterling, VA: Stylus, 1999.

Gates, Henry Louis, Jr. *Loose Canons: Notes on the Culture Wars.* New York: Oxford University Press, 1992.

Geiger, Roger. "Organized Research Units: Their Role in the Development of University Research." *Journal of Higher Education* 61 (1990): 1–19.

———. *Research and Relevant Knowledge: American Research Universities since World War II.* New York: Oxford University Press, 1993.

Getz, Malcolm, John Siegfried, and Kathryn Anderson. "Adoptions of Innovations in Higher Education." *Quarterly Review of Economics and Finance* 37 (Fall 1997): 605–31.

Gibbons, Michael. "Higher Education Relevance in the Twenty-first Century." Paper for the UNESCO World Conference on Higher Education, Paris, France, October 5–9, 1998.

Gleason, Philip. "Minorities (Almost) All: The Minority Concept in American Social Thought." *American Quarterly* 43 (September 1991): 392–424.

Graham, Hugh Davis. *Collision Course: The Strange Convergence of Affirmative Action and Immigration Policy in America.* New York: Oxford University Press, 2002.

Graham, Hugh Davis, and Nancy Diamond. *The Rise of American Research Universities: Elites and Challengers in the Postwar Era.* Baltimore: Johns Hopkins University Press, 1997.

Grant, Gerald, and David Riesman. *The Perpetual Dream: Reform and Experiment in the American College.* Chicago: University of Chicago Press, 1978.

Graubard, Stephen R., ed. "The American Academic Profession." Special issue, *Daedalus* 126, no. 4 (Fall 1997).

Green, Kenneth. "Drawn to the Light, Burnt by the Flame? Money, Technology and Distance Education." *ED Journal* 11 (May 1997): 1–9.

Grubb, W. Norton. "The Effects of Differentiation on Educational Attainment: The Case of Community Colleges." *Review of Higher Education* 12 (Summer 1989): 349–74.

Grubb, W. Norton and Associates, eds. *Honored but Invisible: An Inside Look at Teaching in Community Colleges.* New York: Routledge, 1999.

Gumport, Patricia. "Academic Restructuring: Organizational Change and Institutional Imperatives." *Higher Education* 39 (2000): 67–91.

Gumport, Patricia, and Marc Chun. "Technology and Higher Education: Opportunities and Challenges for the New Era." In *American Higher Education in the Twenty-first Century*, edited by Philip Altbach, Robert Berdahl, and Patricia Gumport, 370–85. Baltimore: Johns Hopkins University Press, 1999.

Hall, Peter. *Inventing the Nonprofit Sector.* Baltimore: Johns Hopkins University Press, 1992.

Harrison, Lawrence, and Samuel Huntington. *Culture Matters: How Values Shape Human Progress.* New York: Basic Books, 2000.

Hawkins, Brian, and Patricia Battin, eds. *The Mirage of Continuity: Reconfiguring Academic Information Resources for the Twenty-first Century.* Washington, DC: Council on Library and Information Resources/Association of American Universities, 1998.

Hearn, James. "Transforming U.S. Higher Education: An Organizational Perspective." *Innovative Higher Education* 21 (1996): 141–54.

Hefferlin, J. B. Lon. *Dynamics of Academic Reform.* San Francisco: Jossey-Bass, 1969.

Henry, William. *In Defense of Elitism.* New York: Doubleday, 1994.

Hirsch, Werner, and Luc Weber. *Governance in Higher Education: The University in a State of Flux.* London: Economica, 2001.

Hoenack, Stephen, and Eileen Collins, eds. *The Economics of American Universities.* Albany: State University of New York Press, 1990.

Hofstadter, Richard. *Anti-intellectualism in American Life.* New York: Knopf, 1963.

Hofstadter, Richard, and Walter Metzger. *The Development*

*of Academic Freedom in the United States*. New York: Columbia University Press, 1955.

Hollinger, David. *Postethnic America: Beyond Multiculturalism*. New York: Basic Books, 1995.

Honan, William. "The Ivory Tower under Siege: Everyone Else Has Downsized, Why Not the Academy?" *New York Times*, January 4, 1998.

Hossler, Don, Jack Schmit, and Nick Vesper. *Going to College: How Social, Economic, and Educational Factors Influence the Decisions Students Make*. Baltimore: Johns Hopkins University Press, 1999.

Hughes, Richard, and William Adrian, eds. *Models for Christian Higher Education: Strategies for Success in the Twenty-first Century*. Grand Rapids, MI: Eerdmans, 1997.

Hunt, Earl. "The Role of Intelligence in Modern Society." *American Scientist* 83 (July–August 1995): 356–68.

Hunter, James Davison. *The Death of Character: Moral Education in an Age without Good or Evil*. New York: Basic Books, 2000.

Hutcheson, Philo. *A Professional Professoriate: Unionization, Bureaucratization, and the AAUP*. Nashville: Vanderbilt University Press, 2000.

Inglehart, Ronald. *Modernization and Postmodernization: Cultural, Economic, and Political Change in Forty-three Societies*. Princeton: Princeton University Press, 1997.

Jencks, Christopher, and Meredith Phillips, eds. *The Black-White Test Score Gap*. Washington, DC: Brookings Institution, 1998.

Jencks, Christopher, and David Riesman. *The Academic Revolution*. New York: Doubleday, 1968.

Johnson, Sandra, and Sean Rush, eds. *Reinventing the University: Managing and Financing Institutions of Higher Education*. New York: Wiley, 1995.

Juhn, Chinhui, Kevin Murphy, and Brooks Pierce. "Wage

Inequality and the Rise in Returns for Skill." *Journal of Political Economy* 101 (1993): 410–42.

Julius, Daniel J., J. Victor Baldridge, and Jeffrey Pfeffer. "A Memo from Machiavelli." *Journal of Higher Education* 70 (March–April 1999): 113–133.

Kaiser, Harvey. *A Foundation to Uphold: A Study of Facilities at U.S. Colleges and Universities.* Alexandria, VA: Association of Higher Education Facilities Officers, 1996.

Kane, Thomas. *The Price of Admission: Rethinking How Americans Pay for College.* Washington, DC: Brookings Institution, 1999.

Kane, Thomas, and Cecilia Elena Rouse. "The Community College: Educating Students at the Margin between College and Work." *Journal of Economic Perspectives* 13 (Winter 1999): 63–84.

Karabell, Zachary. *What's College For? The Struggle to Define American Higher Education.* New York: Basic Books, 1998.

Katz, Richard, and Associates. *Dancing with the Devil: Information Technology and the New Competition in Higher Education.* San Francisco: Jossey-Bass, 1999.

Keller, George. *Academy Strategy: The Management Revolution in Higher Education.* Baltimore: Johns Hopkins University Press, 1983.

———, ed. *The Best of Planning for Higher Education.* Ann Arbor, MI: Society for College and University Planning, 1997.

———. "The Cost—and Price—of Education." *Nation,* March 21, 1970, 242–44.

———. "The Emerging Third Stage in Higher Education Planning." *Planning for Higher Education* 28 (Winter 1999): 1–7.

———. "Examining What Works in Strategic Planning." In *Planning and Management for a Changing Environment,* edited by Marvin Peterson, David Dill, and Lisa Mets, 158–90. San Francisco: Jossey-Bass, 1997.

———. "A Growing Quaintness: Traditional Governance in the Markedly New Realm of U.S. Higher Education." In *Competing Conceptions of Academic Governance*, edited by William Tierney, 158–76. Baltimore: Johns Hopkins University Press, 2004.

———. "Higher Education Management: Challenges and Strategies." In *International Handbook*, edited by James Forest and Philip Altbach, 229–42. Dordrecht, Netherlands: Springer, 2006.

———. "The Impact of Demographic and Social Changes on Higher Education and the Creation of Knowledge." In *Changes in the Context for Creating Knowledge*. ACLS Paper 26. New York: American Council of Learned Societies, 1994.

———. "Increasing Quality on Campus: What Should Colleges Do about the TQM Mania?" *Change* 14 (May–June 1992): 48–51.

———. "The Search for 'Brainpower.'" *Public Interest* 4 (Summer 1966): 59–69.

———. "Six Weeks That Shook Morningside," *Columbia College Today* 15 (Spring 1968): 3–96.

———. *Transforming a College*. Baltimore: Johns Hopkins University Press, 2004.

———. "Trees without Fruit: The Problem with Research about Higher Education." *Change* 17 (January–February 1985): 7–10.

———. "The Vision Thing in Higher Education." *Planning for Higher Education* 23 (Spring 1995): 8–14.

———. *The Wisconsin Idea: Yesterday and Tomorrow*. Madison: Wisconsin Idea Commission, 1986.

———. "Women and the Future of Education." *Futures: The Journal of Forecasting and Planning* 7 (October 1975): 428–32.

Keniston, Kenneth. "Youth: A New Stage in Life." *American Scholar* 39 (1970): 631–54.

Kennedy, Donald. *Academic Duty.* Cambridge: Harvard University Press, 1997.

Kernan, Alvin, ed. *What Happened to the Humanities?* Princeton: Princeton University Press, 1997.

Kerr, Clark. "Speculations about the Increasingly Indeterminate Future of Higher Education in the United States." *Review of Higher Education* 20 (Summer 1997): 345–56.

———. *The Uses of the University.* 5th ed. Cambridge: Harvard University Press, 2001.

Kett, Joseph. *The Pursuit of Knowledge under Difficulties: From Self-improvement to Adult Education in America, 1750–1990.* Stanford: Stanford University Press, 1994.

Kingston, Paul, and Lionel Lewis, eds. *The High-Status Track: Studies of Elite Schools and Stratification.* Albany: State University of New York, 1990.

Kirp, David. *Shakespeare, Einstein, and the Bottom Line: The Marketing of Higher Education.* Cambridge: Harvard University Press, 2003.

Kleinfeld, Judith. "Student Performance: Males vs. Females." *Public Interest* 134 (Winter 1999): 3–20.

Kliewer, Joy Rosenzweig. *The Innovative Campus: Nurturing the Distinctive Learning Environment.* Phoenix, AZ: ACE/Oryx, 1999.

Klitgaard, Robert. *Choosing Elites.* New York: Basic Books, 1985.

Klor de Alva, Jorge. "Remaking the Academy in the Age of Information." *Issues in Science and Technology* 16, no. 2 (Winter 1999–2000): 52–58.

Koblick, Steven, and Stephen Graubard, eds. *Distinctively American: The Residential Liberal Arts College.* New Brunswick, NJ: Transaction, 2000.

Kohl, Kay, and Jules LaPidus, eds. *Postbaccalaureate Futures: New Markets, Resources, Credentials.* Phoenix, AZ: ACE/Oryx, 2000.

Kors, Alan, and Harvey Silvergate. *The Shadow University:*

*The Betrayal of Liberty on America's Campuses.* New York: Free Press, 1998.

Kotter, John. "Leading Change: Why Transformation Efforts Fail." *Harvard Business Review* 73 (March–April 1995): 59–67.

Kouzes, James, and Barry Posner. *The Leadership Challenge: How to Get Extraordinary Things Done in Organizations,* rev. ed. San Francisco: Jossey-Bass, 1995.

Kuh, George, and Associates. *Student Success in College: Creating Conditions That Matter.* San Francisco: Jossey-Bass, 2005.

Kuh, George, and Elizabeth Whitt. *Invisible Tapestry: Culture in American Colleges and Universities.* Washington, DC: George Washington University, 1998.

Kurzweil, Edith, and William Phillips, eds. *Our Country, Our Culture: The Politics of Political Correctness.* Boston: Partisan Review Press, 1994.

Labaree, David. "Private Goods, Public Goods: The American Struggle over Educational Goals." *American Educational Research Journal* 34 (Spring 1997): 39–81.

Lagemann, Ellen Condliffe, *The Politics of Knowledge: The Carnegie Corporation, Philanthropy, and Public Policy.* Middletown, CT: Wesleyan University Press, 1989.

LaNoue, George. "Rethinking Affirmative Action." *Planning for Higher Education* 24 (Fall 1995): 1–8.

Lasch, Christopher. *The Revolt of the Elites and the Betrayal of Democracy.* New York: Norton, 1995.

Lenington, Robert. *Managing Higher Education as a Business.* Phoenix, AZ: Oryx, 1996.

Leslie, David, and Judith Gappa. "Education's New Work Force." *Planning for Higher Education* 22 (Summer 1994): 1–6.

Leslie, Larry, and Paul Brinkman. *The Economic Value of Higher Education.* New York: ACE/Macmillan, 1988.

Levy, Frank. *The New Dollars and Dreams: American Incomes*

*and Economic Change.* New York: Russell Sage Foundation, 1998.

Light, Donald. "The Structure of Academic Professions." *Sociology of Education* 47 (Winter 1974): 2–28.

Lindblom, Charles. *Inquiry and Change: The Troubled Attempt to Understand and Shape Society.* New Haven: Yale University Press, 1990.

Lipman-Blumen, Jean. *Connective Leadership: Managing in a Changing World.* New York: Oxford University Press, 2000.

Lipset, Seymour Martin. *American Exceptionalism.* New York: Norton, 1996.

Lovett, Clara. "How to Start Restructuring Our Colleges." *Planning for Higher Education* 24 (Spring 1996): 18–22.

MacDonald, Heather. *The Burden of Bad Ideas: How Modern Intellectuals Misshape Our Society.* Chicago: Ivan Dee, 2000.

MacTaggert, Terrence. *Restructuring Higher Education: What Works and What Doesn't in Reorganizing Governing Systems.* San Francisco: Jossey-Bass, 1996.

Magat, Richard, ed. *Philanthropic Giving: Studies in Varieties and Goals.* New York: Oxford University Press, 1989.

March, James. "Exploration and Exploitation in Organizational Learning." *Organizational Science* 2 (1991): 71–87.

———. *A Primer on Decision Making.* New York: Free Press, 1994.

Marginson, Simon, and Mark Considine. *The Enterprise University: Power, Governance, and Reinvention in Australia.* Cambridge: Cambridge University Press, 2000.

Marsden, George. *The Soul of the American University.* New York: Oxford University Press, 1994.

Martin, James, and James Samels. *Presidential Transition in Higher Education.* Baltimore: Johns Hopkins University Press, 2004.

Massy, William. "New Thinking on Academic Restructuring." *AGB Priorities* 6 (Winter 1996): 1–16.

Massy, William, and Andrea Wilger. "Improving Productivity: What Faculty Think about It—and Its Effect on Quality." *Change* 27 (July–August 1995): 11–20.

Maurrasse, David. *Beyond the Campus: How Colleges and Universities Form Partnerships with Their Communities.* New York: Routledge, 2001.

Mayer, Susan. *What Money Can't Buy: Family Income and Children's Life Chances.* Cambridge: Harvard University Press, 1997.

McCaughey, Robert. *Scholars and Teachers: The Faculties of Select Liberal Arts Colleges and Their Place in American Higher Learning.* New York: Barnard College/Mellon Foundation, 1995.

McGuinness, Aims. *Redesigning the States' Higher Education Systems for the Twenty-first Century.* Denver: Education Commission of the States, 1993.

McLanahan, Sara, and Gary Sandefur. *Growing Up with a Single Parent: What Hurts, What Helps.* Cambridge: Harvard University Press, 1994.

McPherson, Michael, and Morton Owen Schapiro. "Skills, Innovations and Values: Future Needs for Postsecondary Education." *Change* 27 (July–August 1995): 26–32.

———. *The Student Aid Game: Meeting Need and Rewarding Talent in American Higher Education.* Princeton: Princeton University Press, 1998.

McSherry, Corynne. *Who Owns Academic Work? Battling for Control of Intellectual Property.* Cambridge: Harvard University Press, 2001.

McWhorter, John. *Losing the Race: Self-sabotage in Black America.* New York: Free Press, 2000.

Mead, Lawrence, ed. *The New Paternalism: Supervisory Approaches to Poverty.* Washington, DC: Brookings Institution, 1997.

———. "The Politics of Disadvantage." *Society* 35 (July–August 1998): 72–76.

Menand, Louis. "College: The End of a Golden Age." *New York Review of Books,* October 18, 2001, 44–47.

Metzger, Walter. "The Academic Profession in the United States." In *The Academic Profession: National, Disciplinary, and Institutional Settings,* edited by Burton Clark, 123–208. Berkeley and Los Angeles: University of California Press, 1987.

———. "The 1940 Statement of Principles on Academic Freedom and Tenure." *Law and Contemporary Problems* 53 (Summer 1990): 3–77.

Middaugh, Michael. *Understanding Faculty Productivity: Standards and Benchmarks for Colleges and Universities.* San Francisco: Jossey-Bass, 2001.

Mortimer, Kenneth, and T. R. McConnell. *Sharing Authority Effectively.* San Francisco: Jossey-Bass, 1978.

Murphy, Kevin, and Finis Welch. "Wage Differentials in the 1990s: Is the Glass Half-Full or Half-Empty?" Chap. 12 in *Causes and Consequences of Increasing Inequality,* edited by Finis Welch. Chicago: University of Chicago Press, 2001.

———. "Wage Premiums for College Graduates: Recent Growth and Possible Explanations." *Educational Researcher* 18 (May 1989): 17–26.

Murray, Charles. "IQ, Success in Life, and Inequality: The Ambiguous Merits of Meritocracy." Chap. 11 in *Causes and Consequences of Increasing Inequality,* edited by Finis Welch. Chicago: University of Chicago Press, 2001.

Newman, Frank, Lara Couturier, and Jamie Scurry. *The Future of Higher Education: Rhetoric, Reality, and the Risks of the Market.* San Francisco: Jossey-Bass, 2004.

Nisbet, Robert. *In the Present Age: Progress and Anarchy in Modern America.* New York: HarperCollins, 1988. See esp. chap. 3, "The Loose Individual."

Noll, Roger, ed. *Challenges to Research Universities.* Washington, DC: Brookings Institution, 1998.

Oakley, Francis. *Community of Learning: The American Col-*

*lege and the Liberal Arts Tradition.* New York: Oxford University Press, 1992.

O'Banion, Terry, ed. *A Learning College for the Twenty-first Century.* Washington, DC: American Association of Community Colleges/Oryx, 1997.

O'Brien, David. *From the Heart of the American Church: Catholic Higher Education and American Culture.* Maryknoll, NY: Orbis, 1994.

Ogbu, John. "Cultural Discontinuities and Schooling." *Anthropology and Education Quarterly* 13 (Winter 1982): 290–307.

Oldenburg, Ray. "Making College a Great Place to Talk." *Planning for Higher Education* 20 (Summer 1992): 59–63.

O'Neil, Robert. *Free Speech in the College Community.* Bloomington: Indiana University Press, 1997.

Ong, Walter. *Orality and Literacy: The Technologizing of the Word.* London: Routledge, 1988.

Orton, J. Douglas, and Karl Weick. "Loosely Coupled Systems: A Reconceptualization." *Academy of Management Review* 15 (April 1990): 203–23.

Pascarella, Ernest, and Patrick Terenzini. "Designing Colleges for Greater Learning." *Planning for Higher Education* 26 (Spring 1992): 1–11.

———. "Studying College Students in the Twenty-first Century." *Review of Higher Education* 21 (Winter 1998): 151–65.

Patai, Daphne, and Noretta Koertge. *Professing Feminism: Education and Indoctrination in Women's Studies,* rev. ed. Lanham, MD: Lexington Books, 2003.

Patterson, Orlando. *The Ordeal of Integration: Progress and Resentment in America's Racial Crisis.* Washington, DC: Civitas/Counterpoint, 1997.

———. *Rituals of Blood: Consequences of Slavery in Two American Centuries.* Basic Books/Civitas, 1998. See esp. chap. 1, "Broken Bloodlines."

Pelikan, Jaroslav. *The Idea of the University: A Reexamination*. New Haven: Yale University Press, 1992.

Peterson, Marvin, David Dill, and Lisa Mets, eds. *Planning and Management for a Changing Environment*. San Francisco: Jossey-Bass, 1997.

Poskanzer, Steven. *Higher Education Law: The Faculty*. Baltimore: Johns Hopkins University Press, 2002.

Press, Eyal, and Jennifer Washburn. "The Kept University." *Atlantic Monthly*, March 2000, 39–54.

Privateer, Paul Michael. "Academic Technology and the Future of Higher Education." *Journal of Higher Education* 70 (January–February 1999): 60–79.

Quinn, James Brian, Philip Anderson, and Sydney Finkelstein. "Managing Professional Intellect: Making the Most of the Best." *Harvard Business Review* 74 (March–April 1996): 71–80.

Reich, Robert. *The Work of Nations: Preparing Ourselves for Twenty-first Century Capitalism*. New York: Knopf, 1991.

Resnick, Lauren. "Learning in School and Out." *Educational Researcher* 16 (December 1987): 13–30.

Rhodes, Frank. *The Creation of the Future: The Role of the American University*. Ithaca: Cornell University Press, 2001.

Rice, R. Eugene. *Making a Place for the New American Scholar*. Washington, DC: American Association for Higher Education, 1996.

Riesman, David. *On Higher Education*. San Francisco: Jossey-Bass, 1980.

Roberts, Sam. *Who We Are Now: The Changing Face of America in the Twenty-first Century*. New York: Times Books/Holt, 2004.

Rodriguez, Gregory. "Mexican Americans and the Mestizo Melting Pot." In *Reinventing the Melting Pot*, edited by Tamer Jacoby, 125–38. New York: Basic Books, 2004.

Romer, Paul, and Robert Barro. "Human Capital and

Growth: Theory and Evidence." *Carnegie Rochester Conference Series on Public Policy* 32 (Spring 1990): 251–86.

Roof, Wade Clark. *Spiritual Marketplace: Baby Boomers and the Remaking of American Religion.* Princeton: Princeton University Press, 1999.

Rosen, Sherwin. "The Economics of Superstars." *American Economic Review* 71 (December 1981): 845–58.

Rosovsky, Henry. *The University: An Owner's Manual.* New York: Norton, 1990.

Rosovsky, Henry, and Inge-Lise Ameer. "A Neglected Topic: Professional Conduct of College and University Teachers." In *Universities and Their Leadership,* edited by William Bowen and Harold Shapiro, 119–56. Princeton: Princeton University Press, 1998.

Rothschild, Michael. "Philanthropy and American Higher Education." In *Philanthropy and the Nonprofit Sector in a Changing America,* edited by Charles Clotfelter and Thomas Ehrlich, 413–27. Bloomington: Indiana University Press, 1999.

Rouse, Cecilia. "Do Two-Year Colleges Increase Overall Educational Attainment? Evidence from the States." *Journal of Policy Analysis and Management* 17 (Fall 1998): 595–670.

Ruch, Richard. *Higher Ed, Inc.: The Rise of the For-Profit University.* Baltimore: Johns Hopkins University Press, 2001.

Ruscio, Kenneth. "The Distinctive Scholarship of the Selective Liberal Arts Colleges." *Journal of Higher Education* 58 (March–April 1987): 205–22.

Salomone, Rosemary. *Same, Different, Equal: Rethinking Single-Sex Schooling.* New Haven: Yale University Press, 2003.

Sample, Steven. *The Contrarian's Guide to Leadership.* San Francisco: Jossey-Bass, 2002.

Samuelson, Robert. *The Good Life and Its Discontents: The*

*American Dream in the Age of Entitlement, 1945–1995.*
New York: Times Books, 1995.

Sanford, Timothy, ed. *Preparing for the Information Needs of the Twenty-first Century.* New Directions for Institutional Research Series 85. San Francisco: Jossey-Bass, 1995.

Savage, James. *Funding Science in America: Congress, Universities, and the Politics of the Academic Pork Barrel.* New York: Cambridge University Press, 1999.

Sawhill, Isabel. "The Behavioral Aspects of Poverty." *Public Interest* 153 (Fall 2003): 79–93.

Schier, Tracy, and Cynthia Russett, eds. *Catholic Women's Colleges in America.* Baltimore: Johns Hopkins University Press, 2002.

Schlesinger, Arthur, Jr. *The Disuniting of America.* New York: Norton, 1992.

Schulman, Bruce. *The Seventies: The Great Shift in American Culture, Society, and Politics.* New York: Free Press, 2001.

Schultz, Theodore. *The Economic Value of Education.* New York: Columbia University Press, 1963.

Schuster, Jack, and Martin Finkelstein. *The American Faculty: The Restructuring of Academic Work and Careers.* Baltimore: Johns Hopkins University Press, 2006.

Schuster, Jack, and Lynn Miller, eds. *Governing Tomorrow's Campus.* New York: ACE/Macmillan, 1989.

Seaman, Barrett. *Binge: Campus Life in an Age of Disconnection and Excess.* New York: Wiley, 2005.

Seymour, Daniel. *Once upon a Campus: Lessons for Improving Quality and Productivity in Higher Education.* Phoenix, AZ: Oryx, 1995.

Shaw, Kenneth. *The Successful President.* Phoenix, AZ: ACE/Oryx, 1999.

Shaw, Peter. *The War against Intellect.* Iowa City: University of Iowa Press, 1989.

Shils, Edward. *The Calling of Education.* Chicago: University of Chicago Press, 1997.

Siegfried, John Malcolm, and Kathryn Anderson. "The Snail's Pace of Innovation in Higher Education." *Chronicle of Higher Education,* May 19, 1995, A56.

Simpson, William Brand. *Cost Containment in Higher Education: Strategies for Public Policy and Institutional Administration.* New York: Praeger, 1991.

Skrentny, John. *The Minority Rights Revolution.* Cambridge: Harvard University Press, 2002.

Slaughter, Sheila, and Gary Rhoades. *Academic Capitalism and the New Economy: Markets, State, and Higher Education.* Baltimore: Johns Hopkins University Press, 2004.

Sloan, Douglas. *Faith and Knowledge: Mainline Protestantism and American Higher Education.* Louisville, KY: Westminster John Knox Press, 1994.

Smart, John, Kenneth Feldman, and Corinna Ethington. *Academic Disciplines: Holland's Theory and the Study of College Students and Faculty.* Nashville: Vanderbilt University Press, 2000.

Smith, Charles. *Market Values in American Higher Education.* Lanham, MD: Rowan & Littlefield, 2000.

Sowell, Thomas. *Affirmative Action around the World: An Empirical Study.* New Haven: Yale University Press, 2004.

Sperber, Murray. *Beer and Circus: How Big-Time Sports Is Crippling Undergraduate Education.* New York: Holt, 2000.

Stahler, Gerald, and William Tash. "Centers and Institutes in the Research University." *Journal of Higher Education* 65 (September–October 1994): 540–54.

Stark, Joan, and Malcolm Lowther. *Strengthening the Ties That Bind: Integrating Undergraduate Liberal and Professional Study.* Ann Arbor: University of Michigan School of Education, 1998.

Steele, Claude. "Race and the Schooling of Black Americans." *Atlantic Monthly,* April 1992, 68–78.

Steele, Shelby. *The Content of Our Character.* New York: St. Martin's, 1990.

Stimpson, Catherine. "Women's Studies and Its Discontents." *Dissent* 43 (Winter 1996): 67–75.

St. John, Edward P., and Michael D. Parsons, eds. *Public Funding of Higher Education: Changing Contexts and New Rationales.* Baltimore: Johns Hopkins University Press, 2004.

Stone, Melissa, and Candida Brush. "Planning in Ambiguous Contexts." *Strategic Management Journal* 17 (1996): 633–52.

Suro, Roberto. *Strangers among Us: How Latino Immigration Is Transforming America.* New York: Knopf, 1998.

Taylor, Charles. *The Ethics of Authenticity.* Cambridge: Harvard University Press, 1992.

Thernstrom, Stephan, and Abigail Thernstrom. *America in Black and White: One Nation Indivisible.* New York: Simon & Schuster, 1997.

Tierney, William. *Building the Responsive Campus: Creating High Performance Colleges and Universities.* Thousand Oaks, CA: SAGE Publications, 1999.

Townsend, Barbara, and Susan Twombly. *Community Colleges: Policy in the Future Context.* Westport, CT: Ablex Publishing, 2001.

Traub, James. *City on a Hill: Testing the American Dream at City College.* Reading, MA: Addison-Wesley, 1994.

Trow, Martin. "Admissions and the Crisis of American Higher Education." In *Higher Education for Everybody? Issues and Implications,* edited by W. Todd Furniss, 26–52. Washington, DC: American Council on Education, 1971.

———. "American Higher Education: Exceptional or Just Different?" In *Is America Different? A New Look at American Exceptionalism,* edited by Byron Shafer, 138–86. Oxford: Clarendon Press, 1991.

———. "American Higher Education: Past, Present and Future." *Educational Researcher* 17 (April 1988): 13–23.

———. "Reflections on the Transition from Mass to Universal Higher Education." *Daedalus* 99 (Winter 1970): 1–42.

Turner, Paul Venable. *Campus: An American Planning Tradition.* Cambridge: MIT Press, 1984.

Twigg, Carol. "The Impact of the Changing Economy on Four-Year Institutions of Higher Education: The Importance of the Internet." Chap. 3 in *The Knowledge Economy and Postsecondary Education: Report of a Workshop,* edited by Patricia Graham and Nevzer Stacey. Washington, DC: National Academy Press, 2002.

Van Alstyne, William, ed. *Freedom and Tenure in the Academy.* Durham: Duke University Press, 1993.

Vedder, Richard. *Going Broke by Degree: Why College Costs Too Much.* Washington, DC: AEI Press, 2004.

Walberg, Herbert. "Families as Partners in Educational Productivity." *Phi Delta Kappan* 65 (February 1984): 397–400.

Wattenberg, Ben. *Fewer: How the New Demography of Depopulation Will Shape Our Future.* Chicago: Ivan Dee, 2004.

Welch, Finis, ed. *The Causes and Consequences of Increasing Inequality.* Chicago: University of Chicago Press, 2001.

Wildavsky, Aaron. *Craftways: On the Organization of Scholarly Work.* 2nd ed. New Brunswick, NJ: Transaction, 1993.

Wilson, James Q. *On Character: Essays.* Washington, DC: AEI Press, 1991.

———. *The Moral Sense.* New York: Free Press, 1993.

Wilson, William Julius. *The Truly Disadvantaged: The Inner City, the Underclass, and Public Policy.* Chicago: University of Chicago Press, 1987.

Winston, Gordon. "The Positional Arms Race in Higher Education." Discussion Paper 54, Williams Project of the Economics of Higher Education, Williams College (April 2000).

———. "Subsidies, Hierarchy, and Peers: The Awkward

Economics of Higher Education." *Journal of Economic Perspectives* 13 (Winter 1999): 13–36.

Wolfe, Alan. "The Feudal Culture of the Postmodern University." *Wilson Quarterly* 20 (Winter 1996): 54–66.

Wolverton, Mimi, and Larry Penley. *Elite MBA Programs at Public Universities: How a Dozen Innovative Schools Are Redefining Business Education.* Westport, CT: Praeger, 2004.

Wong, Frank. "Pilgrims and Immigrants: Liberal Learning in Today's World." *Liberal Education* 71 (Summer 1985): 97–108.

Young, Michael. *The Rise of the Meritocracy, 1870–2033: The New Elite of Our Social Revolution.* New York: Random House, 1959.

Zimbalist, Andrew. *Unpaid Professionals: Commercialism and Conflict in Big-Time College Sports.* Princeton: Princeton University Press, 2001.

# INDEX